T0283322

BORN
TO BE
BRAVE

BORN
TO BE
BRAVE

HOW TO BE A PART OF AMERICA'S
SPIRITUAL COMEBACK

KIRK CAMERON

Post Hill
PRESS

A POST HILL PRESS BOOK,
published in cooperation with Brave Books

Born to Be Brave:
How to Be a Part of America's Spiritual Comeback
© 2024 by Kirk Cameron
All Rights Reserved

ISBN: 979-8-88845-423-7
ISBN (eBook): 979-8-88845-424-4

Cover design by Cody Corcoran
Cover photo by Samira Bouaou
Interior design by John D. Ziner

Post Hill Press
New York • Nashville
posthillpress.com

Published in the United States of America
5 6 7 8 9 10

To the memory of Dr. Marshall E. Foster

Contents

Contents

God did not give us a spirit of timidity,
but a spirit of power, of love and of self-discipline.

—THE APOSTLE PAUL, 2 TIMOTHY 1:7

Foreword

by Pastor Jack Hibbs

In an age when cowardice is cloaked as compassion, license disguised as love, and bold and blatant sin is called bravery, we have never more needed clarity than now. No two ways about it—we are at a crossroads. To some, it may seem the battle is lost, the hill too steep, time too short, and the faithful too few. But to those who know the truth, the need for the moment is finally coming into focus. The moment desperately needs brave, unwavering men and women, holding fast to the truth, wearing love, true love, like a banner, standing firm on the only Rock that cannot be shaken. This is the moment we were made for. And in the immortal words found in the Book of Esther, "Who knows but that you have come to your position for such a time as this."

It is no surprise that our nation seems desperate for revival. A cursory look at the facts surrounding mental health, happiness, job satisfaction, relational connection, confidence in our political leaders, etc., will affirm what we already sense in our souls: what we've got isn't working. The American church stands at the precipice of the most important decision in modern history: boldly cling to, proclaim, and rely on the truth or buckle. Put another way, the choice is this:

choose freedom, life, and liberty, or sacrifice those things on the altar of comfort, political correctness, and convenience.

Born to Be Brave is unquantifiable in its importance. The truth relayed in these pages is necessary for every American Christian, every individual concerned about the "spiritual state of the union," and any person who is concerned about our future. What our nation needs is not a conservative president (though that would help), a stronger military (though that would be wise), or a more sure economy (though that would be nice) but rather the presence and participation of bold and faithful people keen to the wisdom of the "good way, where life is." Thank God, the result of faithful men and women adhering to the truth will undoubtedly result in the transformation of neighborhoods, cities, states, eventually countries, and even the world. What starts in the heart of one man or woman does not stay there. The fact of the matter is that we don't need quick fixes from Pennsylvania Avenue; truly the answer will not be coming from the White House, the State House, nor from Wall Street, or Hollywood, but from God's house.

What we need is one man, one woman, you.

Born to Be Brave speaks directly to the heart of the concerned but convicted, the perplexed yet passionate, the one who has not yet lost hope. It accurately assesses the reality of our times but gives us the path to spiritual revival, practical reformation, and the change we long for. It has been said that "The only thing necessary for the triumph of evil is for good men to do nothing," and we must step into our God-given purpose and begin doing "something." Our hopelessness is misplaced. The fact is, our heritage as a nation, and more so as a faith family, is one of impressive, eternal, sure hope, and it is time to start living it out.

For me, Kirk has proven himself over the decades to be a man who is committed to the Word of God and to the history of this nation that we call America. It is this country, unlike any other in the history of man, which had its origins with God, in the Word of God, by the hand of God. My years of ministry have enjoyed numerous occasions where Kirk and I would serve together in outreaches and presentations on the wonderful reality of God in our American story. Kirk Cameron is a man who walks in obedience to the Word of God. I have personally witnessed him be a man of integrity and a Christian who lives out his faith in a beautifully winsome, bold, and loving manner. Together, he and I have often spoken up and out on issues that threaten not only the security of our nation but the education of our children and even our churches. Kirk has become the tip of the spear in the United States for his passion to reclaim our lost and willfully ignorant public school educational system. This latest work by Kirk Cameron is no surprise to me. He has always proven himself to be a trustworthy man of integrity, who loves his family, but above all, loves his God. I want to commend the reading of this book to you, as it will no doubt shape your biblical worldview and the nation that you live in. The very nation in which God, according to Jeremiah 29:7, has placed you to be a light and to be an influence for righteousness.

Born to Be Brave challenges us to be warriors, but also reminds us of our call to bear the truth in love, be filled with compassion, and be unsurprised when the world hates or persecutes us. The Gospel is the way to eternal life, but it also has real-world, daily implications that lead to life and blessing in every corner in which it is applied. We know the end of the story is a resoundingly victorious one, but we must step up to play our parts. If enough of us stepped up to the plate, we could start a moral and spiritual awakening. We are told that we are given everything we need for life and godliness, that our identity is one of power, courage, and victory, and that we stand on the shoulders of saints, warriors, and prophets who have gone before us. This is our spiritual heritage.

D. L. Moody has said, "A revival means days of heaven upon earth." Kirk and I are confident that these days are ahead of us.

It is time to stop allowing the opposition to have the final word, because we know the final word. May you do more than read; may you be transformed by the truth in these pages. May you be inspired to "take up arms" with confidence that the "living God" is on your side. America's story is not over; our King is on the move. You were *Born to Be Brave*.

Jack Hibbs, Senior Pastor of
Calvary Chapel Chino Hills and
President of The Real Life Network

CHAPTER 1

The Setup

When principles that run against your deepest convictions begin to win the day, then battle is your calling, and peace has become sin; you must, at any price of dearest peace, lay your convictions bare before friend and enemy, with all the fire of your faith.

—ABRAHAM KUYPER

I fitted on a bulletproof vest while glancing out the windows of my parked security van at the crowd of protestors who had taken up position outside a public library in Washington, DC. Activists from the LGBTQ+ community were shouting and waving homemade signs with messages attacking me and the fellow authors I was with for a reading event. One large female was shouting obscenities through a bullhorn at everyone who came near. The DC police leadership were taking this situation seriously enough that they had dispatched half a dozen officers to the scene to prevent violence.

I don't mind admitting I was nervous.

This was the end of March 2023, and I was halfway through a monthslong book tour, reading my children's books at libraries around the country. On this day, at DC's Cleveland Park Library, I was going to read my book *As You Grow*, designed to encourage development of the fruit of the Spirit through the seasons of life. It would seem that a kids' book promoting love, joy, peace, and other such virtues could hardly be controversial. But apparently *I* was controversial because of things I'd said about my faith and some current social issues. And so a disruption force from the Alphabet Army was in place to try to make this book reading uncomfortable for me and the other presenters and the family participants.

In planning this book tour, my publisher and I selected libraries that had already invited drag queens to lead story hours for children. We were intending to test the libraries' commitment to free speech: Would they let a conservative Christian like me hold an event in their public reading rooms? At first all the libraries rejected me… until I went on Fox News and let it be known that I was prepared to go to court to assert my constitutional right to free speech. Suddenly, all the libraries let me sign up to lead a story hour. But that doesn't mean the librarians liked it. Nor did many of the leftists living in those cities. I started touring anyway.

We had seen hate-filled protestors at most of my readings, but so far neither I nor the families who had come out for the events had been harmed by any of it, at least not physically. In DC, though, the risks were higher, this being the epicenter of American progressivism. Most worryingly, the Trans Radical Activist Network had designated the following day as Trans Day of Vengeance. (How such an event made any sense in the wake of the Covenant School shooting that had taken place earlier that week in Nashville, committed by a trans shooter, I can't tell you.) I remember thinking, *Could this be the one that will make me sorry I'm doing this?*

A four-man executive protection team (bodyguards) were present to escort me and my three fellow authors into the library. In advance, the security firm had prepared a six-page threat assessment for this event, and the guards possessed schematics of the library, identifying a safe room and an escape route from the building. The van driver had a map of the quickest route to a hospital emergency room.

These precautions were not an overreaction, any more than the presence of the police was an overreaction. Tension was at a peak, and the possibility of violence was real. In fact, only a few days later the swimmer Riley Gaines had to be rushed to *her* safe room when transgender activists physically assaulted her at a speaking event. Thankfully, though, when my team made its move, the worst that happened outside the library was that the shouting and cursing reached a crescendo. We all made it safely into the building.

Once inside, we encountered the "welcome" that the librarians had prepared for us. Specially for this day, they had put up rainbow flags, transgenderism flags, and displays of LGBTQ-themed books for kids and teens, including such titles as *My Princess Boy* and *I'm Not a Girl*. The library was sending a message that, even though they couldn't stop me and the other conservative authors from being there, they didn't approve of us—they were in solidarity with the progressive side.[1]

It's not surprising that our audience was smaller at Cleveland Park Library than at other locations on the tour. To get to my reading, parents would have to take their children through the same experience I'd had: expose them to the shouted vulgarities and threatening gestures of the protestors outside, then make them pass through the LGBTQ+ propaganda. It could be scary and confusing for kids, and could potentially even be dangerous. Some would-be attendees no doubt saw what was going on and turned around for home. And yet dozens of moms, dads, and kids refused to be frightened away, and we all had an enjoyable story time despite everything.

At most of the book reading events on the tour, we had hundreds and even thousands of participants. And over and over again at these events I saw the same thing happen: people weren't as fascinated by Kirk Cameron, former star of the TV show *Growing Pains*, as they were by each other. You could see it on their faces that they were thinking, *Where did all these people come from?* Moms or dads would come up to shake my hand and then would say things like "I had no idea so many in my town are interested in promoting positive values instead of the usual immoral and backward stuff we're supposed to just accept."

Because so many people came out for most of these events, some unfortunately had to wait a long time for a chance to enter the reading room, and this created some of the most beautiful moments. In at least two libraries I can recall—those in Scarsdale, New York, and Indianapolis, Indiana—parents and grandparents invited children to sit in circles in the aisles while the adults read aloud books of virtue to them. In Scottsdale, Arizona, the crowd spontaneously started singing worship songs, such as "Amazing Grace" and "Jesus, We Love You," the music reverberating throughout the atrium. Local sheriff Mark Lamb was in attendance, beaming at the crowd. I was brought to tears. For me it was like watching a revival going on inside this public building, despite the homelessness, crime, and other problems that sadly were going on outside on the city streets.

Listen to me now. I'm from Hollywood, the land of make-believe, where we create perceptions that have little to do with reality. It's all designed to make you believe something, to make you feel something, to get you to do something. And the same kind of deception is being practiced on the whole nation by the leaders of wokeness, who want to make the family of faith run a gauntlet of fear so they can neutralize us and replace our God-given values and freedoms with their own domination of affairs.

But perception is not reality.

If you believe in God, value liberty, and don't appreciate the new morality being pressed upon you, then you can be sure there have been people behind the scenes trying to make you believe you're an antiquated relic, one of a handful of unreconstructed cranks whose time has gone. It's not true. This perception is not reality. As the attendees at the library events discovered, there are hundreds, thousands, millions of people—not just in a few regions but even in the most progressive parts of the country—who believe in the timeless values that produce blessing and protection for us and for our children.

The question is, what we are going to do with this realization?

Second-Birth Bravery

As the father of six now-grown children, I love kids, and I'll continue to write kids' books. But I had to interrupt the writing of my young-reader series in order to write *this* book for adults. Because the nation needs our help *right now.*

At this point, I believe, I could easily inflame your anger with facts and stories about things happening in our society that are an offense to faithful and liberty-loving people across the land: from out-of-control government spending that threatens our financial future, to untamed political corruption, to the redefinition of marriage, to the ongoing slaughter of the unborn, to racial divisiveness under the guise of social justice, to parents being cut out of their kids' life-altering decisions, to the loss of free speech on university campuses, to much, much more.

I *could* get into details on all this, but I bet you already know about it as well as I do. You get a reminder every time you skim the news headlines.

As pervasive and serious as they are, the current problems of society are *not* the most acute reasons that the message of *Born to Be Brave* is needed right now. Instead, this book is critical today because the family of faith in America is standing at a crossroads of decision. As I see it, we could go one of two ways from this point. If we choose the first path, we get comfortable with being a minority group and become resigned to having less and less influence in the culture, marching toward abject tyranny. If we take the second path, we decide once again, as believers have done repeatedly in our national past, to take the lead in shaping society to conform more closely with biblical principles for the honor of God, the flourishing of the family, and the advantage of all citizens.

There's no guarantee we *won't* take the easy road toward irrelevancy. The once-vibrant churches in Western Europe are today seen by many as little more than depositories of tradition and centers for do-goodism; it's not hard to imagine American Christianity devolving into the same. But in America it's not too late—perhaps *just barely* not too late—for the second alternative of choosing to reassert our values within our own homes and the public realm.

What will make the difference in which way we go? Not more outrage about the state of our culture, but a firmer grip on who we are in Christ and why we were born.

All human beings have potential for courage from the cradle merely by virtue of being made in the image of God. But the bravery I'm talking about comes from *the second birth*, where we are born "not of natural descent, nor of human decision or a husband's will, but born of God" (John 1:13). This courage is not for a few believers but is a quality that *every person within the family of faith* can and should exhibit. If we struggle with cowardice, that is a leftover of our old selves; it is not a part of the new creation God has made of us through His grace.

As I define it, second-birth bravery is *doing what is right so that God's will may be done and good may prevail, regardless of the cost to ourselves*. It's got everything to do, then, with the *purpose* behind the bravery, and that's what sets it apart from the daring acts of terrorists who blow themselves up or gang members who jeopardize their lives in the conduct of their crimes. It's not even the same thing as taking a risk to better one's own lot or provide for loved ones, though there's usually nothing wrong with that kind of courage. Second-birth bravery comes out of an understanding that God has chosen us to represent Him and pursue His desires wherever we are. Deep in our souls we know that, if we want to participate in the transformation of the world for the sake of God and of good, we can't do it without bravery.

So, are we living that way?

As I look around at the family of faith, what I see is that many of us are fearful and cringing in the face of what seems an overwhelming opposition. We're feeling intimidated—exactly as some people want us to feel. So much scorn and censure have been directed at us that we've begun to second-guess ourselves, wondering whether it is even right to suggest that biblical values could be relevant in public decision-making. Naturally enough, we don't want ourselves and our families to have to pay costs for standing up for unpopular beliefs. We're discouraged. We're plain scared.

I'm not singling anyone out or accusing you of anything, but I'm reminding all of us—myself included—that bravery is meant to be *normal* for us. The most encouraging thing about this is that bravery isn't something we have to somehow manufacture within ourselves. It's less about our natural grit than about God's supernatural gift. Through the new birth, He's already placed the capacity for tremendous courage within us, and we just need to access it and live it out.

Lion within Lion

In Disney's *The Lion King*, the evil lion, Scar, kills the rightful king, Mufasa, and takes his place ruling the Pride Lands.[2] Scar also chases away Mufasa's young son and heir, Simba.

Years pass and Simba grows up living a heedless *"hakuna matata"* life with his friends at their desert oasis. Eventually Simba's mate, Nala, tries to convince him to return to the Pride Lands and set things right. But Simba refuses. He'd rather stay where he is, leading a pleasant if insignificant life, rather than take the risks involved with challenging injustice.

Then a mandrill monkey named Rafiki (a kind of prophet figure) shows up to change Simba's mind. Wisely, Rafiki doesn't try to engage Simba's bravery by telling him how bad things have gotten back at the Pride Lands. Instead, he reminds Simba of his own special identity.

> RAFIKI: You don't even know who you are.
> SIMBA: Oh, and I suppose you know.
> RAFIKI: Sure do. You're Mufasa's boy.

Then Rafiki leads Simba to a pool of water where he can observe his reflection. At first Simba sees only himself. But soon he realizes that he's staring at his father's image. "See," comments Rafiki, "he lives in you."

The reflected Mufasa delivers the message Simba needs to hear: "You have forgotten who you are and so have forgotten me. Look inside yourself, Simba. You are more than what you have become.… Remember who you are."

Today's society is in bad shape, but our primary motivation for activating our bravery is not the need for change. Our primary motivation is the honor of our Father in Heaven. What enables and empowers us to be brave is not primarily a response to danger but the spirit of power, love, and self-discipline that flows as we embrace our true identity in Christ.

Remember who you are.

You are a child of God. You bear the Father's image. Since long before we got into the present cultural setback, He intended for you to take a bold part in advancing His will in the world. In fact, as Ephesians 1 says, God chose you *before the creation of the world*, predestining you for adoption as His child and revealing to you the mystery of His will—"to bring all things in heaven and on earth together under one head, even Christ" (verses 3–10).

In *The Lion King*, when Simba finally returns to do battle with Scar, the usurper looks at Simba running toward him and at first thinks he sees the father. Scar cries out in horror, "Mufasa! No, you're dead."

It's the same with us. When the destroyers of liberty and those who have wrought immoral changes in our society spot us coming, they should see the image of our Father in us.

The Biggest "What If...?"

Could I ask you a question—one that, frankly, I want you to not just think about but *memorize, repeat to yourself, and share with others?* Because I believe it has the potential to transform our fears into hope and put our feet on a very different path than the one we may have been following up to this point.

> *What if the present cultural setback*
> *is really a divine setup*
> *for a spiritual comeback*
> *led by the family of faith?*

Maybe the things that today are making us disgusted about our society aren't merely the way it is, an unfixable brokenness created by people's poor choices. Maybe God has secretly been at work within our cultural turmoil, embedding an opportunity few can see. It's not about one political philosophy prevailing over another, because if that were so, a political party would be all that's needed to bring about change. Instead, this is an opportunity custom-made for the family of God and dependent on the miracle power of God. A renewal that's potentially bigger than any ever witnessed in our lifetime—transforming not just hearts but the entire culture—might be nearer than we've ever considered possible. This could be the family of faith's finest hour.

Before we can take advantage of the setup within the setback, however, we have to shed the prevailing Christian mindset about the future of our culture: that things are inevitably going to get worse. We may think that way because there's so much doom in the headlines (doom gets clicks, folks), or we may expect things to get worse because we believe that these are the "last days" and that in the last days society is going to go down the tubes. These are some things I'll be getting to later in the book. But regardless of how you're feeling or what your long-term prognosis for the world might be, if it means you're underestimating the power of God to act in the present circumstances, you're making a mistake. If you think God's given us a pass on doing all we can to represent His values in our time, that's dishonoring to Him. If you don't believe there's an opportunity here—a setup for a comeback—I want to suggest it's time to open your eyes of faith.

We *can* be a part of a change in souls and society that will extend the heavenly influence of the Kingdom far beyond what we see today. We just need a recovery of our newborn spiritual identity with its birthright to bravery.

Let me tell you more about a friend of mine whom I've already briefly mentioned. Riley Gaines was faced with a dilemma and chose to resolve it with faith and courage.

Making a Splash Outside the Pool

Born into a sports-loving family in Tennessee, Riley early on committed herself to the sport she loved most—swimming. And she worked hard at it, putting in the thousands of hours in the pool that it took to make her a standout swimmer in high school and earn a place on the women's swim team at the University of Kentucky.

When her senior year at Kentucky came around in 2021, Riley's goal was to become a national champion. Her hopes were looking realistic halfway through the season, when she was ranked third nationally in her top event, the 200-meter freestyle.

Curiously, though, the swimmer who was ranked fifth in the 200 free, and first in the 500 free, was a person no one on Riley's team had heard of before: Lia Thomas. The collegiate swimming world was not so big, and the people at the top tended to know one another. So, who was this?

A few days after the competitor's nation-leading times were posted, an article came out that cleared up the mystery. Lia Thomas was formerly Will Thomas and swam three years on the men's team at the University of Pennsylvania before switching to the women's team.

Competing on the men's team, Thomas had been a mediocre swimmer at best, ranking 554th in the 200 freestyle and 65th in the 500 freestyle. Now, competing as a female, Thomas had leaped into the top five places in both events.[3] Whenever anyone tried to claim that this sudden achievement could all be put down to the training Thomas had been doing since transitioning, their words rang with falseness.

Thomas's inclusion in women's competitions was outrageously unfair to all those who had come up through the female swimming system since childhood. Furthermore, how could it be right that women as young as eighteen should have to share a locker room with

Thomas? At this point, Riley was sure someone who was supposed to be protecting the female swimmers—a coach, an official, an administrator—would stand up for her and the others. Shamefully, no one did.

At the championship meet held in March 2022, Riley came up against Thomas in the 200-meter freestyle. In the finals they tied for fifth. Two swimmers touching the wall at exactly the same time is an unusual occurrence in this sport, and it created an awkward—but revealing—situation.

"So we go behind the awards podium," recalled Riley afterward, "and the NCAA official looks at both Thomas and myself, and he says, 'We don't really account for ties, so we're gonna give this trophy to Lia.'"

Riley was told to pose with the sixth-place trophy, and afterward she was required to give the trophy back. She went home empty-handed, while Lia Thomas took the fifth-place trophy home.

Often, in the course of becoming brave, there's a specific turning point that makes all the difference, the energizing of one's God-given courage. That's how it was with Gaines. She said, "When this official reduced everything that I'd worked my entire life for down to a photo op to validate the feelings and the identity of a male at the Women's National Championship, that's when I was done waiting for someone else to speak up."[4]

Others were trying to portray the inclusion of trans athletes in sports as being safe and fair, but now Gaines was ready to tell the truth. And she did.

"I can wholeheartedly attest to the tears that I saw from the ninth- and seventeenth-place finishers who missed out on being named an All-American by one place," said Gaines in an interview. "And I can wholeheartedly attest to the extreme discomfort in the locker room when you turn around and there's a six-foot-four biological male dropping his clothes, exposing male genitalia, watching you and other girls undress."

Originally having planned for a post-collegiate career in dentistry, Riley deferred that goal to become an activist for women's safety, privacy, and equal opportunities. She has traveled the country speaking on these subjects and has testified before the US Senate, US House, and several state legislatures. She also joined me at one of my library reading events in 2023.

Her name is widely recognized today, but don't miss this—once she was just another college swimmer, unknown outside her sports and personal circles. An "ordinary" person, if you want to put it that way. But even if she never became a celebrity of sorts, she had already become extraordinary by making the brave choice to speak up and tell the truth.

Imagine America

If the present cultural setback really is a divine setup for a spiritual comeback, then dream with me about what might lie ahead if we are like Riley and we start to live out the courage we've been designed for since ages past.

Imagine an America where people who have suffered the emptiness and brokenness of rejecting God turn to Jesus, by faith, and are filled with His presence.

Imagine an America where Christians who have been unfaithful to the Lord, or whose love for Him has grown cold, repent and become fiery with the Holy Spirit.

Imagine an America where fear of man gives way to confidence in God.

Imagine an America where love floods in to occupy the spaces burned out by hate.

Imagine an America where the presumption that Christians should keep their faith to themselves is replaced by a consensus that the happiest societies are those based on a love for God and His Word.

Imagine an America where we stop the tide of illegal immigration at the border, while welcoming legal immigrants and refugees to a flourishing nation based in godly beliefs and traditions.

Imagine an America where racial and cultural communities, instead of being set against one another, live side by side in that beautiful *e pluribus unum* way.

Imagine an America where privately owned business is encouraged and celebrated, with personal and corporate integrity supported by limited government oversight, and where the shadow of socialism has passed away.

Imagine an America where we don't have to fight for legislative and court victories with regard to preborn life, marriage, parental rights about education, and the like, because our civil representatives and the majority of Americans are already with us.

Imagine an America where the oppressiveness of the woke police and their commitment to cancel others give way to a love for free speech and civil discourse among the people.

Imagine an America where the government shrinks to something more appropriate in size and cost because individuals, families, churches, and communities are taking more responsibility for themselves and saying no to government handouts.

These may seem like impossibilities to some—but they are not. I want you to hear me loud and clear: these things are not only possible but they are *inevitable* and *unstoppable* when believers get a grip on their newborn identity and begin to apply, with courage, the simple strategy outlined in this book.

It's Yours If You Want It

I'm no longer leading a movement to restore wholesome book readings to public libraries. Not because I've tired of it or given up on it, but because I don't need to do it anymore—others are carrying on the work.

Among the thousands of people who attended my story hours were many who caught the vision for what I was doing. If they wanted good books to be read to their kids at libraries, all they had to do was pursue that goal themselves. They just had to exercise their bravery and insist on their God-given and Constitutional rights. Rooms full of families praying, singing, and reading books of virtue and character are the result. This may not be the kind of thing that's going to get headlines in mainstream journalism, but to me it's *beautiful*.

Now, *you* may not feel called to read books for kids, and that's absolutely fine. But you may be concerned about your school board's decisions that harm children, or local politicians promoting family-unfriendly events, or efforts to defund and hinder the police, or any number of other causes. Or you may not yet know where you should get involved. Either way, I hope this chapter has begun to stir a sense in you that God wants to use you *somewhere* in a way you are uniquely positioned and equipped for.

Intimidation tactics by anti-Christian foes don't have to succeed. The threatening Greta Thunberg scowl that radical progressivism is fixing on you right now doesn't have to paralyze you. Whoever wants the culture more is going to get it, and all we're missing is a standard operating procedure of faith and courage that is directed toward the desires of God for our families and our nation.

Sometimes we can suffer real harm when we enter into the cultural fray. I can't deny it. Other times, though, as when I stepped out of the security van in DC to face protestors and opponents, it turns out that many of our enemies bark but they don't bite. Rather than giving up, let's simply pray for God to restrain the dangers so we can continue on the course He has called us to. Providence favors the brave.

What if the present cultural setback is really a divine setup for a spiritual comeback led by the family of faith? I believe with all my heart that it is. And the next question we need to ask is this: Is the family of faith ready to take advantage of the divine setup? If we will put our complacency and cowardice behind us, then there's no reason why we can't. This book is about the why's and how's of preparing for the nationwide, maybe *global*, transformation that we so desperately need.

Are you brave enough to go there with me?

CHAPTER 2

Heavenizing Earth

Jesus's resurrection is the beginning of God's new project not to snatch people away from earth to heaven but to colonize earth with the life of heaven. That, after all, is what the Lord's Prayer is about.

—N. T. WRIGHT

Today's "social justice warriors" and progressive extremists have swept through our culture, leaving burnt-out neighborhoods, schools in tatters, and moral wastelands, and now they fully intend to occupy the positions of power and fulfill their vision of a new socialist-humanist America. And what about us people of faith, or anybody who just wants their families to be able to live in freedom? Tough for us. We're supposed to bow down to the new hierarchy of moral authority, accept the changed social environment, and fall in line with the "elites" who know better than we do.

I've said this *setback* may be a hidden setup for a *comeback*. Referring to this comeback, I'm not just talking about climbing back to some kind of equal standing with the woke, sharing power and making compromises with them. And I'm not talking about recovering what was lost or even "taking back America," although in some ways it may look like that. I'm talking about the opportunity for a transformation of America where divine wisdom, instead of worldly thinking, decides our ways, creating conditions that enable all citizens to share in the blessings that descend.

I really believe this is possible. For one thing, I have faith. For another, it's happened before.

Let me take you back more than a millennium to Britain of the ninth century. The Gospel had come to the island much earlier, during the Roman occupation, and by the ninth century most Britons were Christian at least in name. But Britain's Christian identity and liberty were now under threat, because Viking longboats kept showing up on the shores, spilling out warriors who had come not just for hit-and-run raids but to conquer and rule. These Norse invaders were pagans who practiced polytheism, sacrifice, and sorcery. To them, peaceful Britain looked ripe for plucking. They pillaged, torched, and butchered their way through this island, city after city, dominion after dominion, destroying families, religious practices, and cultures.

Until, that is, the Vikings came to the south-central kingdom of Wessex—the most powerful kingdom in the patchwork of realms that made up Great Britain at that time.[1]

For seven years, King Alfred of Wessex and his army held back Guthrum the Viking and the heathen horde that was intent on conquering Britain. But eventually the Viking strength of arms became too much for them. On the twelfth day of Christmas, in January 878, Alfred, together with his family, was driven out of his home, barely preserving his life. He took shelter on a tiny island in a swamp, where as a boy he had learned how to hunt with his father.

He could have made a strategic retreat to the mainland of Europe for safety and liberty, but he didn't do that. Instead, he stayed in Wessex to stand with his people and fight for liberty and truth, eventually moving to a secret base on top of the highest hill in his kingdom to observe the movements of Guthrum and the Viking army.

Meanwhile, most of the people of Britain thought Alfred was dead and they had no champion left. They were under the heavy yoke of Viking tyranny. Their women were raped, their men were murdered, and their property was plundered, seemingly without any recourse. Life in Britain had become miserable, hopeless.

It's not hard to imagine that Alfred himself may have struggled with discouragement at this stage. Some may have advised him to give up, because the Viking wave seemed unstoppable and destined to engulf all of Britain. But Alfred prayed and asked God for courage. He wasn't done yet.

With a small band of warriors, Alfred began to take out the Viking scouts and cut off their supply lines. Gradually, news filtered out to the people that they still had a king who sought their liberty. Then Alfred sent a message secretly to the men of the land, calling them to gather for one more battle against Guthrum the Viking.

Five weeks after Easter, on the day of Pentecost in May 878, Alfred made his way through the forest to the rendezvous and found five thousand men committed to the cause. They were overjoyed, as though they had just seen their king come back from the grave. Alfred equipped them with weapons and, more importantly, with hope. The devout Alfred exhorted them, "Men, be faithful to God no matter the outcome, and He will be faithful to you."

At the chosen battle site, before a Viking-occupied fortress, Alfred had his men form a shield wall to march on the enemy. Alfred locked himself in with the others and led the attack toward Guthrum and the Viking warriors, who formed their own shield wall. The

Vikings arrogantly believed they would destroy the Britons without great trouble, but Alfred's men had everything to lose—their children, their property, their future—and so they were unrelenting and determined.

It was a clash of shields, with at first neither side making much of an impact on the other. The Viking army included berserkers, a body of shock troops who were filled with drugs and demonic dedication as they would leap over Alfred's shield wall, only to be impaled by his soldiers' spears. Even they were unable to give their side an advantage.

Finally a break opened in the Viking shield wall. Alfred swiftly led his men into the opening to begin hand-to-hand combat. The battle became a bloodbath. Both sides suffered terrible losses, but the men of Wessex gained the upper hand.

Guthrum, the Viking leader, escaped and hid in his fortress with other survivors from his once-proud army. But Alfred and his men quickly surrounded the fortress, and Guthrum realized he had no choice but to either surrender or starve to death. Within days, he gave himself up.

The customary practice at this point would have been for Alfred to drag Guthrum and his fellow Viking leaders into the open and behead them one by one. What Alfred did instead constituted one of the greatest public acts of mercy of the age. He offered to spare Guthrum's life if the Viking would agree to convert to Christianity, be baptized, and sign the Treaty of Wedmore, which would allow Guthrum to rule over a portion of Britain while obligating him to treat all the citizens of his kingdom equally, whether they were Saxon or Scandinavian.

Guthrum was so grateful to Alfred that he went along with the plan. He was baptized and became a son of Alfred in the faith. This former Viking invader would remain an ally to King Alfred in battle for the rest of his life. His devotion was so thorough that when

Guthrum minted his coins, he had not Guthrum but Athelstan—
the Christian name Alfred had given him—engraved on them.

This is what second-birth bravery achieved in ninth-century
Britain. Bravery has always been a game-changing quality, even if our
generation has nearly forgotten how important it is. And what I want
to emphasize is the *transformation* that this victory, under a wise and
godly leader, brought to the entire land.

Society Remade

After Alfred had neutralized the immediate threat by Guthrum,
he began to rebuild Wessex and eventually all of the Anglo-Saxon
kingdoms. He wanted to recover the best of Roman-era British
Christianity. Furthermore, he had a vision of what Britain could
turn into in the future if it were comprehensively redesigned around
biblical principles, with peace, justice, and prosperity sought for
everybody in the land.

He built walled cities, established a standing army, and created
a naval force that could challenge the Viking longboats before they
landed on England's shores. He constructed new church buildings
and appointed faithful church leaders to replace the corrupt ones. He
sought out top scholars from all over Europe, founded a court school,
and encouraged learning. The church, the arts, and the economy all
flourished under his leadership.

Alfred believed the Vikings were a scourge sent by God to wake
up his people, who had fallen into spiritual apathy, and he believed
the future of his country depended on systemic revival, especially at
the local level. He said, "Local government ought to be synonymous
with local Christian virtue; otherwise it becomes local tyranny, local
corruption and local iniquity."[2] Alfred's task, his greatest goal, was to
help rebuild the Christian virtue and wisdom of his people, starting
at the grassroots.

Consistent with this aim, Alfred revised the law code of Wessex, rooting it in Scripture and Christian tradition. He began with his own translation of the Ten Commandments from Latin to English, then included other passages from the Law of Moses, applying them to English society in his day. After this, he followed up with excerpts from Jesus's Sermon on the Mount. He concluded with a brief history of the growth of Christian law among the Christian nations.

Alfred understood that a well-ordered and virtuous society needed more than just the enforcement of wise laws; it needed redemption of the human heart. In his preface to his law code, Alfred quoted the Golden Rule: "Do unto others as you would have them do unto you." He then wrote, "If a man understood how to apply this one law alone he would need no *domboc* [law book]."[3]

Alfred's body of law became the foundation for what we now know as English common law, and then later in the United States, our Constitution and Bill of Rights. The concept of equal rights under God can largely be traced back to King Alfred.

One historian said of him, "He was a fierce warrior, a devout Christian, ever thirsting for wisdom, deeply committed to justice, a lover of mercy, and a king who gave himself for his people. He was practically a myth and a much-needed reality."[4] He is also an inspiration for us today, reminding us that, even when circumstances seem hopeless, it is possible to reverse harmful trends in society and reorient a nation around godly truths and values, bringing good to all.

I call this *heavenizing earth*, and it's what all believers should be doing. The term can seem unrealistic, even presumptuous, but don't forget—it's the very first thing that Jesus, in His model prayer, told us to be asking for.

Our Father in heaven,
hallowed be your name,
your kingdom come,

your will be done
on earth as it is in heaven.
(MATTHEW 6:9–10)

After His resurrection, Jesus gave orders to get to work on this project. Because He possessed "all authority in heaven and earth," He told His followers, "Go therefore and *make disciples of all the nations*, baptizing them in the name of the Father and of the Son and of the Holy Spirit, teaching them to observe all things that I have commanded you" (Matthew 28:19–20, KJV, emphasis added). Note that this is not just about making individual disciples within the nations but making disciples of the nations themselves. Furthermore, teaching the nations to "observe all things whatsoever I have commanded" includes commands that affect public and personal life.[5]

This is so much more than electing a president, seating "our kind" on the Supreme Court, or winning a few battles in a culture war. It's making earth more like Heaven, starting right where we are.

False Binaries

There are some ways in which I'd like to restore binary thinking in present Western culture, like the idea that God made the human race in two distinct genders and that's a good thing, as Genesis 1 says. Or that there's a real difference between truth and error, not just a bunch of baseless moral "constructs" that come and go.

In other ways I want to *challenge* binary thinking, because I think there are several mental distinctions that members of the faith family need to overcome if we are going to engage our culture. They are things we have separated though God has joined them together. God's vision is ultimately about bringing the binary of *Heaven and earth* closer together.

Sacred versus Secular

People use the word *secular* a lot, referring to a secular vocation, a secular college, and so on. But if by "secular" people mean that God and faith don't have anything to do with a certain area, they've got too small a vision of God's reign. "The earth is the Lord's, and everything in it, the world, and all who live in it" (Psalm 24:1). That's comprehensive, as I read it.

Abraham Kuyper, a theologian and prime minister of the Netherlands more than a century ago, put it unforgettably: "There is not a square inch in the whole domain of our human existence over which Christ, who is Sovereign over all, does not cry, Mine!"[6]

The problem with viewing some areas of our experience as "secular" and not essentially Christian is that it causes us to compartmentalize our lives, with faith present in some boxes but absent from others. This flies in the face of New Testament commands like this one: "Whatever you do, whether in word or deed, do it all in the name of the Lord Jesus" (Colossians 3:17).

The statement *Jesus is Lord* is our most basic confession, and it is absolute. Jesus is Lord of our hearts. Jesus is Lord of our marriages and families. Jesus is Lord of our churches. Jesus is Lord of our schools. Jesus is Lord of our clubs and friend groups. Jesus is Lord of our companies. Jesus is Lord of the economy as a whole. Jesus is Lord of our political parties. Jesus is Lord of the justice system. Jesus is Lord of the military. Jesus is Lord of Congress and the White House. Jesus is Lord of the universe. Jesus is simply Lord, no exceptions.

We never enter into any arena of life where God is not in charge or where our faith should not apply. It's all sacred.

Spiritual versus Physical

There's a real distinction to be made between the spiritual and the physical, but we can get into all kinds of wrong-headedness if we think that our faith is connected only with the spiritual and not with the physical. That misguided thinking goes back to Greek philosophy, not to the Hebrew-Christian Scriptures.

In the Ten Commandments, the first four commandments are God oriented, while the final six are others oriented (Exodus 20:2–17). Our worship *and* our relationships should be God honoring. Both the consecration of our hearts and the condition of our community life matter to Him.

When a Jewish Bible scholar asked Jesus which was the greatest commandment in the Hebrew Scriptures, Jesus wouldn't limit Himself to one. He named two: *love God* and *love your neighbor* (Matthew 22:35–40). If we just read our Bible, and pray, and go to church, and evangelize, but don't actively show practical love to others, then our love and obedience are falling short. Our active love might mean helping another person privately, like the good Samaritan did to the wounded man, but it extends as well to more public actions. It includes working to influence policies and laws for the good of others, as Joseph, Daniel, and so many other people of faith have done.

God cares about everything in the physical, visible world around us, and so should we.

Church versus State

Regrettably, the often-heard phrase "the separation of church and state" has been the source of much misunderstanding. Many are surprised to learn that it does not appear anywhere in the Declaration of Independence or the Constitution of the United States. In fact, it comes from a letter Thomas Jefferson wrote in 1802 to a group of Baptists where Jefferson was describing his position on the First Amendment.[7]

It might be most useful to ask, then, what does that amendment itself say?

The First Amendment's reference to religion has two parts. The first says, "Congress shall make no law respecting an establishment of religion." In other words, America wasn't going to have a national church, like England and most other countries in the Old World had. Different denominations of Christians had taken root in different states, but the national Congress wasn't going to privilege any of them.

The second part says that Congress shall make no law "prohibiting the free exercise" of religion. Government has to keep its hands off its citizens' religion. And the amendment doesn't restrict the meaning of that exercise to church matters or divide it from issues affecting the state. People are free to exercise their faith in all matters of public interest, and the government shall not interfere.

Your Constitutional birthright includes personal spiritual practices conducted at home or with your fellow believers in church gatherings, but you're also free to vote for candidates for reasons of your religious beliefs, to advocate for public policy based on biblical principles, and to exercise your faith publicly in other ways as you see fit. Let me ask you something: Although the Constitution doesn't stand in the way of the free exercise of your faith, *do you?* Too many of us have internalized a certain idea of "the separation of church and state" to a point where we unnecessarily divorce our faith from critical areas of life.

Contrary to what the godless say, what most Christians today need is *freer* exercise of religion. Sacred or secular, spiritual or physical, church or state, we should exercise our faith freely and boldly, without apology! And if we don't, we can be sure someone else will.

The Myth of Neutrality

Consider the glory of a religiously pluralistic society:

Once, the great majority of Americans were Christians, at least in name, but anybody who thinks this is still a Christian country is stuck in the past. Not that Christians aren't still welcome—they are, if they play by the rules. But they don't run the show anymore. We have plenty of Jews, Muslims, Hindus, Buddhists, and others here. Not to mention the growing numbers of people who don't identify with any religion and who may be atheists or have some kind of individual belief in God. Thank God (if God exists) we have religious liberty so that each group can do its own thing in its own place of worship. And meanwhile the separation of church (mosque, synagogue, temple…) and state guarantees that civil government and law shall stay free from religious influence. Thus we can all go on with a public life that does good and treats everybody equally.

Isn't that a beautiful thing?

To some people, it is. And it certainly contains some truth. But in its essence it is deceptively *false*. Civil government isn't and never will be religiously neutral. Nature abhors a vacuum, and likewise culture will inevitably follow the lead of one worldview or another. Sooner or later, *someone's* values will dominate in the public square.

Multiculturalism is not a worldview; it's a transitional stage between one orthodoxy and another. And there's little mystery about what new orthodoxy American society is headed toward. Unless things change, we aren't moving from a Christian-oriented worldview toward a religiously neutral society; we're moving from a Christian-oriented worldview toward a humanist culture. One puts Christ at the center, while the other puts humanity at the center.

Many promote the idea of a religiously neutral public life because they genuinely believe it's possible and good. But a lot of today's humanist leaders are more sophisticated than that, and more cynical, and when they bring forward the idea of neutrality, it's really as a tactic to clear the ground so that they can move in and take over with their brand of religion.

Secular humanism is a totalizing philosophy. What I mean is that people on the woke-socialist-atheist side want to completely dominate the culture and government of the United States. The progressives don't want to meet you at the fifty-yard line and say, "Hey, let's sit down right here and be friends." They want to push you back until you're in your own end zone and they own the field.

It may seem contradictory, but secular humanists are actually trying to heavenize earth too. It's just that, for them, this involves creating a socialist utopia on earth. All such totalizing movements and philosophies are really *counterfeits* of God's authentic call to heavenize earth under the authority and in the name of Jesus. Social critic Russell Kirk said that the conservative "thinks of policies as intended to preserve order, justice, and freedom. The [progressive] ideologue, on the contrary, thinks of politics as a revolutionary instrument for transforming society and even transforming human nature. In his march toward Utopia, the ideologue is merciless."[8] That's why the Left keeps coming up with such crazy things as mutilating surgeries for children and economic laws that devastate a family's ability to provide for themselves.

Unlike the leftist revolutionaries, Christian conservatives should not try to remove other people's liberties. The spiritual comeback that I believe lies ahead will bring with it *more* freedom, not less, and in fact it is the *only* solid hope that this will happen. Just as Christianity birthed the modern rights of freedom of speech and freedom of religion, so also is Christianity the best guarantor that those rights will survive, for everyone. On the other hand, if you sever the root of Christianity, the fruit of freedom will wither.

At the same time, freedom of religion doesn't mean all religions are equal. The man-made *First Amendment* is put into perspective by the divine *First Commandment*: "You shall have no other gods before me" (Exodus 20:3). In America we're free to choose in matters of faith, but we can choose either poorly or well. May we have the wisdom to choose to follow Christ and be His hands and feet to transform culture in such a way that God is honored and all people benefit.

In that light, let me extend an invitation to you....

Welcome Back to the Culture

I wonder if you've noticed something: lots of Christians today, in knee-jerk fashion, talk about the culture in a negative and hopeless way. *We've lost the culture. The culture is so filthy now. I just want to keep my kids safe from today's culture.*

I admit I've carelessly said some things like this. Maybe you have too.

It's like we've abandoned culture, or at least segregated ourselves into a little ghetto of the great metropolis of the larger culture. So the time is past due to remember that, biblically speaking, culture is our calling.

God's earliest instructions to the human race were these: *rule over all the earth* (Genesis 1:26) and *fill the earth and subdue it* (verse 28). The idea of *ruling over* and *subduing* (or *taking dominion over*, in some translations) shouldn't be taken as inciting violence and destruction. It's really about using the raw materials God put in the world and making them into things that are useful or lovely. Adam's work gardening Eden (2:15) is an example of this kind of subduing. Out of this mandate spring agriculture, construction, sculpture, music, poetry, dance, manners, cooking, acting, and so many other human endeavors that give life richness and meaning. While filling the earth is about *colonizing* God's world with human beings, subduing it is about *culture*.

And if God commanded us to create culture, we've got to stop looking at culture as if it is inherently bad. In fact, culture is inherently good. (The "fill" and "subdue" commands of Genesis 1:28 are specifically placed within a context of God's blessing.) Of course, like anything humanity has touched since the curse of Genesis 3, our culture making has a mix of evil in it. When people use culture to promote racism, demean people made in the image of God, or interfere with God's intentions for marriage and the family, for example, then it *is* subduing in the destructive sense. The potential for harm calls for discernment, separating bad from good, false from true, ugly from beautiful; it *doesn't* mean we should give up on culture. God has never canceled His command to make good things and behave in ways that improve life for the human race, any more than He's told us to stop having children.

Believer, you are called not to ban the culture but to build the culture. Be brave enough to find out where you can engage with and contribute to what's going on in society, rather than withdrawing from it. To the extent that you reflect the truth and goodness of the Creator God, you are making the earth a little more like Heaven. And if someone criticizes you for dragging your religion into the common culture, tell them they're doing the same thing.

The poet T. S. Eliot said culture is our "lived religion."[9] In other words, culture is nothing more than what's inside the hearts and minds of people showing up on the outside. Whatever you believe about God or ultimate meaning will be reflected in what you create or express, and that's as true for atheistic humanists as it is for Christians, Muslims, Hindus, and people of other religions. "Dragging in your religion" is not a faux pas; it's the whole thing.

I hope we, as Christians, will be intentional in how we live out our faith in all spheres of life. It isn't about engaging in a culture war. It's about boldly, freely, joyfully expressing what we know and have experienced of God and God's ways. It's about being blessed and being a blessing to others.

Don't give up on culture. Give up on the idea that you don't have the right to contribute to culture or respectfully respond to others' contributions to culture. Give up on the fear of what could happen to you if you dare to play on the field of culture. Give up on the belief that the people of faith can't have a transformative influence on culture, making life better for all.

The culture is yours.

Better Book Fare

Almost every adult living today who went to school in the United States has at least one shared memory, and that's buying Scholastic books. The company has always had some great books for sale, including the Clifford the Big Red Dog series and the Stuart Little series, along with a lot of lesser-known educational and fun reads. Back in the 1970s, when I went to school in the San Fernando Valley, I loved filling out an order form for books like *James and the Giant Peach* and *The Mouse and the Motorcycle,* along with choose-your-own-adventure books.

Scholastic book fairs started in the 1980s. Eventually they spread until more than 120,000 public schools per year, or more than 90 percent of the nationwide total of schools, were hosting these fairs. Kids bought Scholastic books in vast numbers, or even if they didn't, they still had access to them because many of the same titles made it onto the shelves of the school libraries.

But in recent years the Scholastic book fairs have changed in a disturbing way. Along with a lot of good books, the company is now pushing books that indoctrinate readers in dark and morally twisted ideology or make a mockery of traditional American values. Young kids today are likely to come home with stories about gay dinosaurs, transitioning toddlers, and cross-dressing ducks. For older kids, Scholastic's offering includes books promoting critical race theory, books with explicit language and occult overtones, and books with illustrations bordering on the pornographic.

Many parents, particularly parents of faith, have been concerned about this change but have shrugged and said, "There's nothing we can do about it." After all, Scholastic controls the culture of in-school book buying.

But some friends of mine and I had a different idea: What if we could give schools another book fair option besides Scholastic? One that offers a wide range of valuable books while weeding out the morally degrading content and sexually confusing ideologies? And SkyTree Book Fairs was born.

After my campaign to get positive and wholesome books read aloud to kids in public libraries, the SkyTree alternative seemed like a natural follow-on. In that same vein I'm also working on a new TV show for kids called *Adventures with Iggy and Mr. Kirk*—think Mr. Rogers with high-tech animation and an iguana puppet character. And who knows what might be next after that? I can't tell you where any of it will go, but I share these personal examples as a reminder that we don't have to be passive about an ungodly culture, even if that culture seems entrenched. We can take our place in culture where previously it seemed we were not wanted.

The Original Occupy Movement

Many of us remember all too well the Occupy movement that started on Wall Street in 2011 and spread to hundreds of locations worldwide over the next few years. Occupy protestors supposedly represented the lower "99 percent" of the population, angry at the dominance of the top "1 percent." They took over whole neighborhoods, disrupting lives and businesses and often creating destruction and leaving chaos behind them, all with dubious success in elevating the condition of the poor. But I guess it was fun for the occupiers and made them feel good about themselves.

I wonder if any of the protestors knew that Jesus set in motion another Occupy movement a long time ago, with far greater goals than modern-day leftist activists have ever conceived.

Then again, I also wonder how many Christians know about it.

It started in those electric days when Jesus was going to Jerusalem for the last time, with the city filled with pilgrims for a festival. The crowds were all stirred up about Jesus—but they didn't get what He was really up to. "The people thought that the kingdom of God was going to appear at once" (Luke 19:11).

This is exactly the reason why many Christians today aren't bothering to try to heavenize earth, as I'm going to explain in more detail in a later chapter. "Jesus is coming back soon," they say, and until then they believe they're not going to get anywhere with changing a doomed culture, so why waste energy trying?

Jesus knew the people were mistaken about what was about to happen. He wasn't going to overthrow the Roman Empire and bring in the messianic kingdom right then. He was going to die on a cross, rise again, and then appear to a limited number of His followers before disappearing into the clouds. There was going to be a delay until He brought in the kingdom in the most complete sense. In the meantime Jesus couldn't allow the do-nothing, let's-just-wait-for-Jesus-to-return attitude to stand. He wanted His followers to *work* while He was gone. Therefore, as He so often did when He wanted to communicate to the masses, He told a story.

In this story (Luke 19:12–27), a nobleman gathered ten of his servants and distributed a substantial sum of money to each of them, instructing them to invest the money while he was away on a trip. In an older translation, the nobleman said to the servants, "Occupy till I come" (verse 13, KJV). In other words, *Take charge of my wealth while I'm gone. Do business with it. Make my funds grow, and expand my influence in this place, despite my absence.* This investment talk might reflect too much of a capitalist perspective for some people's taste today, but this was what Jesus said.

Sometime later, the nobleman (now elevated to royalty) returned home and checked in with his servants about the investments they'd made on his behalf. However much of a return the servants reported, the king praised them, entrusting them with more wealth in proportion to how well they'd done—a tenfold reward for a tenfold return on investment, fivefold for fivefold, and so on. But what I want to point out is something that made the king really mad.

One servant had done nothing to grow the money he had been given. All that time the master was away, this servant didn't bother to "occupy" anything. He'd just held on to the asset he'd been given; he'd failed to earn capital gains, or even interest, on it.

Why not? He explained to the king, "I was afraid of you" (verse 21). He lacked faith and courage. He lacked *bravery*.

And right here is where we need to ask ourselves how the story connects with us.

The basic code of this parable is easy to crack, as Jesus intended.

+ The nobleman/king = Jesus.
+ The servants = us.
+ The money = all our Heaven-sent gifts and opportunities for doing good on earth in Jesus's name.
+ The trip = Jesus's absence from earth after He ascended into Heaven.
+ The king's return = the Second Coming and judgment.

Right now, we are foot soldiers in our own Occupy movement—not Antifa thugs in face masks but representatives of Christ pursuing a peaceful agenda of good. With every opportunity Christ gives us, we're to spread the good news about His kingdom throughout the world. We're to be brave—and *busy*—until all the nations walk in its light and the kings of the world enter in all their glory (Revelation 2:4).

This isn't cultural agitation for the purpose of economic redistribution played out for the benefit of the TV cameras to advance a political agenda. It's spiritual and cultural transformation for the good of the whole world, and each of us servants of God has a part to play in it.

It's heavenizing earth.

Not So Exotic

It's not often that I get to watch a pastor performing a striptease on stage at church—but it happened once. Sort of.

I'd better give the background before I go any further with this.

In the spring of 2020, as COVID-19 spread across the land, individuals, businesses, and governments began to react. Sometimes *over*react. Predictably, my deep-blue California began enacting some of the most draconian measures in the nation.

On March 19, Governor Gavin Newsom issued a statewide stay-at-home order. Churches, among other places of public gathering, would have to close, because they were "nonessential." Most pastors felt badly about closing the doors of their churches, but it was unclear where this pandemic was going, and of course no one wanted to be responsible for spreading a serious disease, so they complied. At least one pastor, though, quickly began to have second thoughts.

Rob McCoy, senior pastor of Godspeak Calvary Chapel of Thousand Oaks, was a former mayor of that town and was still holding a seat on the city council when COVID struck. Knowing the body of Christ was ordained by God and not ultimately under the control of state government, he decided that his church had to at least open for services during Holy Week, in April. Even though the church took careful precautions for those services—sanitizing seats, requiring masks, letting members into the building ten at a time, and distancing them twenty-five feet apart—the church was still technically in violation of the law. After Easter, the church closed again.

But then, in late May, Black Lives Matter riots broke out across the country, bringing people together in large, mostly unmasked, and presumably contagion-spreading groups. In Los Angeles, the activities of the rioters included blocking freeways, throwing rocks at vehicles, looting stores, vandalizing Jewish neighborhoods, and attacking police officers. And Governor Newsom—the same politician who in his wisdom closed the churches—*gave the riots his support.*[10]

"We knew then that the restrictions had nothing to do with the virus," Pastor McCoy recalled. "So, we opened—wide open."[11]

Government reaction against the Thousand Oaks church inevitably followed, with threats of legal action and the imposition of fines eventually amounting to hundreds of thousands of dollars. At one hearing McCoy told a judge, "I'll see the inside of a jail cell before you'll see a penny of that money."[12] The biblical presumption is that God's people will obey the human authorities, as long as those authorities are standing against bad conduct and leaving the people free to engage in good conduct (Romans 13:1–7). Every once in a while, though, we may feel God calling us to share in the spirit of the apostles when they said, "We must obey God rather than men!" (Acts 5:29). This was one of those moments.

Pastor McCoy was never arrested, the fines were never collected, and the church was never forcibly closed.

Meanwhile, attendance at the church tripled. Why? Because people detected the perfume of freedom wafting from that church.

Christians from closed churches switched over, and many non-Christians who were feeling the pain of isolation and restriction showed up to see what would drive Christians to gather in defiance of civil authority. Here was an instance of Christians taking the lead in pursuit of liberty, exactly as it should be.

I was one of those who started coming to services at Godspeak, and that's why I was in the congregation one Sunday in late 2020 when striptease music began to play and Pastor McCoy came out and started a mildly exotic dance.[13] As we all knew from the news, the California court system was giving exemptions for strip clubs to open, and Pastor McCoy was having a little fun while pointing out the absurdity of declaring churches "nonessential" when strip joints were "essential." He claimed that his dance transformed Godspeak temporarily into a strip joint, thus making it legal to open.

I'm grateful that Pastor McCoy helped to bring a little heavenly freedom to southern California at a time when the authorities were abridging civil rights in an outrageously biased manner.

I'm also grateful he removed only his tie.

Pastor McCoy took a lot of flak for his positions regarding the government's COVID response. I got a taste of the same thing later that year when I was criticized for organizing outdoor Christmas caroling events and beachside campfire singalongs where we declared that masks were voluntary. In our own small ways—and while having fun doing it—we challenged governmental choices that had made life worse for the whole population.

As all of us continue to face a culture under stress, God may choose to send another Alfred the Great—a standout historical figure who will unite God's people and lead them in a giant leap forward in the heavenizing of earth. But I don't think we should be waiting for that to happen. Instead, we should be asking how *we* can move things forward and display some of that Alfred spirit ourselves. You and I *are capable of this*. We were *born for it*.

Jesus said that, beginning in His day, "the kingdom of heaven has been forcefully advancing, and forceful men lay hold of it" (Matthew 11:12). This reflects what John the Baptist and Jesus were achieving by faithful effort, along with the way that the crowds responded by swarming them, almost like an invading army attacking a fortified city. Jesus wasn't condemning this forcefulness. He was commending eagerness for the things of God.

Heavenizing earth shouldn't be a rare, exotic act. It should be an everyday choice for the brave-born.

CHAPTER 3

Reporters and Reformers

*It is not the critic who counts: not the man who points out how the
strong man stumbles or where the doer of deeds could have done
better. The credit belongs to the man who is actually in the arena,
whose face is marred by dust and sweat and blood, who strives
valiantly, who errs and comes up short again and again, because
there is no effort without error or shortcoming, but who knows the
great enthusiasms, the great devotions, who spends himself in a
worthy cause; who, at the best, knows, in the end, the triumph of
high achievement, and who, at the worst, if he fails, at least he fails
while daring greatly, so that his place shall never be with those cold
and timid souls who knew neither victory nor defeat.*

—THEODORE ROOSEVELT

As I've traveled the country and met with all kinds of people in
churches, schools, libraries, and homes, I've noticed that they
contain two types of people. There are *reporters* and there are *reformers*.

By *reporters*, I'm *not* referring to journalists, that is, literal
reporters. I'm talking about the huge numbers of us who spend a lot

39

of our time "reporting" to each other about developments we see in our present period of cultural setback. Actually, a better term might be *repeating*, because all we're really doing is passing on news bits, whether accurate or flawed, fresh or stale, consequential or trivial. But usually alarming. "Look what they're doing over there." "Those guys are corrupt." "That's blatant hypocrisy!" "Have you heard about this new evil that's happening?" "You'll never guess what law they just passed in such-and-such a place."

This bad habit usually starts with excessive news consumption and doomscrolling, often without digging into context or comparing sources. We just position ourselves to be triggered and go straight to outrage. Then while we're still feeling hot about it, we text a link to a friend, or post about it on social media, or corner our friends and family and try to get them as worked up as we are. And we're sure to include our own take on what it all means.

Reporting might make us feel proud of ourselves, because it enables us to demonstrate that we are too clever to accept mainstream culture's spin on the truth—we call a spade a spade. But is reporting *good*? Not usually. It reinforces our negativity bias, making it harder for us to be objective the next time. Meanwhile, it increases our stress, anxiety, and fear, and it transmits the same negative emotions to others. In other words, we're making it harder for everyone to be brave. What a nice gift to give!

I'm not trying to stop you from watching the news (though cutting back may be a good idea for you). I'm just trying to get you to move beyond having an emotional reaction to current events. I don't want to leave you on your couch, bemoaning the state of society and crying in your Chick-fil-A soup, then reaching for your phone to text someone who will sympathize. I'm trying to get you to *do something*.

If we're going to see a spiritual comeback in our day, a lot of us are going to have to make the move from mere reporting to active reforming. We've got to stop being complainers and whiners and turn into creators and winners. To use Jesus's metaphors, we must embrace our roles as the salt of the earth, preserving what otherwise would rot, and the light of the world, showing the way to others through the darkness (Matthew 5:13–16).

There's no time to waste, because while we delay *reforming* society to better reflect the kingdom of Heaven, others are already busy *deforming* it according to humanistic, if not demonic, ideologies.

Deformers

Transgenderism often leads its victims to mutilate their bodies, sometimes starting in childhood. The "gender-affirming care" provided by our medical system has been called the new lobotomy, because like that discredited medical practice (slicing through the brain with a scalpel to try to relieve mental illness), "gender-affirming care" is barbaric, destructive, and doesn't resolve the underlying issues. Trans people who take powerful hormones or go under the knife are accepting irreparable damage to the good bodies a good God gave them. And all of this is done to try to perfect what can never be more than an illusion.

I'm not intending to single out transgender people for criticism, because we all choose unwise paths in life at times. In fact, let me say that I feel deep compassion for people with gender dysphoria, wanting them to find solutions that will meet the real needs of their souls. For their sake, I hope the new lobotomy will go the way of the old one. But I bring up the transgendered because the mutilation some of them choose for their bodies is the perfect metaphor for the whole program of the godless in our day. The humanistic agenda is *deforming* our traditions, our values, and our ways of life. I'm talking about…

+ Judicial activism that reads into the Constitution protections for evil and punishments for the good
+ Deliberate attempts to shift institutions like the family, education, and civil government off their Christian foundations
+ A revisionary view of history that magnifies vices and minimizes virtues in the past
+ A distaste for the rule of law that shreds our borders and creates death and mayhem on our streets
+ The relocation of responsibility for children from their parents to schools and government agencies
+ Sexuality divorced from marriage
+ America's proud military services misused for social tinkering
+ Discouragement of self-reliance and encouragement of victimhood
+ Biased "fact checking" used to short-circuit free self-expression
+ The casual transference of the debt we have incurred to our children and grandchildren
+ Willingness to deny the right to life to those least capable of defending themselves

Such trends are nothing new: deformers have been at work throughout American history. For example, John Dewey, a socialist, atheist, and signatory of the Humanist Manifesto, followed the example set by Horace Mann and in the early twentieth century tried his best to scrub biblical teaching as well as parental influence from US public schools. At the time he was active, American public education, though certainly not perfect, was nevertheless like a flourishing tree. And for a while after our schools became systematized, professionalized, and de-Christianized, the tree continued to look healthy...but at the root it had a disease that continued to sicken the tree. That sickening has grown worse until our public education has become what it is today: hostile to Christianity, resistant to parental leadership, controlled by government bureaucrats and the teacher's union, used as a center for promoting woke ideology and permissive morality. Today's progressives wouldn't be fighting so hard over education if they didn't understand it is determinant for America's future.

Similar deformation processes have occurred, and are still occurring, in many areas of society.

This deforming of America is the reason we need to get busy reforming. And I'm talking specifically to the family of faith here, because to bring about lasting change, this reforming had better go much deeper than politics.

Conservatism Without the Gospel

I like listening to smart people who possess experience and insights I don't have. I pay attention to experts from both ends as well as the middle of the political spectrum, though my own conservative convictions are settled, and so naturally I find more affinity with conservative speakers. I especially enjoy listening to people like Jordan Peterson, Dennis Prager, Ben Shapiro, and some of the more thoughtful right-wing politicians and academics.

But there's something I've realized over time, and I think it's a crucial point that a lot of my fellow conservatives have never considered before: *conservatism without the Gospel doesn't work.*

It never has been, and never will be, possible to truly reform the culture apart from the power of the Gospel. Why? Because we can have great principles and great policies, effective fundraising, advantageous alliances, big media buys, and clever political strategies, but without transformation of the heart, you and I are still stuck in Adam's prison. We're slaves to sin, unable to live up to our own ideals, and so any attempt we make to restructure society and clean up culture, even if based on solid ideas, is never good enough to give more than partial or temporary relief.

Scripture tells of many occasions when God's people responded to national problems, such as a threat by a foreign power, by relying on their own wisdom and strength, trying to make savvy political or economic decisions for pragmatic reasons. God didn't say to them, "Nice effort! I like to see you trying." No, He said, "You fools! Your number-one move should have been to turn to me for wisdom and obey my commands. I will fight your battles. I will guide your steps."[1]

Here is where we have a huge advantage over the godless who oppose us—in a way, our *only* advantage. If we're doing it right, we're not ultimately relying on our own power and smarts. We're not trying to produce a human solution. Instead of depending on our performance, we're relying on God to bring about supernatural results. We're trying to get on His side, instead of hoping He'll get on ours, or ignoring Him altogether.

Heavenizing the earth can't be just a euphemism for colonizing a bunch of people who reason like we do. This is not you and me going out there and getting this done through our wit and grit, but rather, really, it has got to be the work of the Spirit in and through us. "The only thing that counts is faith expressing itself through love" (Galatians 5:6).

Without the Gospel, we're like Paul and Silas in the Philippian prison (Acts 16:16–40). They could pray and sing hymns to God, but they didn't transform the jailer, his household, and the larger society until God sent a great earthquake to shake the foundations of the prison and throw open the doors. Then they could go out and heavenize the earth—such a revolutionary transformation that it was seen even in their own day as *turning the world upside down* (17:6, KJV).

What we need here in America are not just good ideas that build on the best of America's past, though I pray that we will have more and more of those kinds of ideas. More importantly, we need a spiritual earthquake to shake us, throwing open the doors and setting us free from the bondage of sin and shame, guilt and fear, and give us the power to proclaim the Gospel. Then we can implement good ideas systemically, holistically, and comprehensively, so that we are in alignment with the ways of God.

True reformers are products of the Gospel themselves. Men and women with reformed hearts reform their world. People who have been reformed in their heart by the power of the Holy Spirit lead with the Gospel.

It's natural, because God Himself is a reformer and not just a reporter.

The Spiritual History of Ceaseless Reform

Think of the time long ago, in Noah's day, when society had gotten a lot worse than it is today. "The Lord saw how great man's wickedness on the earth had become, and that every inclination of the thoughts of his heart was only evil all the time" (Genesis 6:5). *Only evil all the time.* I wonder what that could even have looked like? On second thought, I'm not sure I want to know.

There's one thing I'm sure of: the Father was not up in Heaven having a staff meeting with the Son and the Holy Spirit, saying, "Look at that! Did you see what they're doing? Can you believe that? And after all we've done for them…. Well, I guess we'll just have to let it go." No. He deployed His own Great Reset, dealing with the out-of-control sin problem by sending the Flood. It was drastic reform, but then the situation called for drastic. The Flood put a stop to mankind's runaway train ride to destruction.

After the Flood, it was like creation started all over again: Noah's family began to be fruitful and multiply, replenishing the earth and taking dominion for the honor of God. Reform had begun.

God used His people to reform again and again throughout history, whenever needed.

He used Abraham to reform the salvation path of the world by founding the chosen family of faith.

He used Moses to reform a broken, defeated people into a functional nation and to reform the basis of law.

He used David to reform with a model of kingliness and a dynasty that would culminate in the Messiah.

He used the prophets to call the people to reform and change countless times, though the people would often not open their ears.

Jesus *reformed humanity itself* by giving us a new heart with new desires. And yet it didn't stop there. Throughout Christian history, as we have done "even greater things" than Jesus through the power of the Spirit (John 14:12), the reform has just kept on coming.

For example, by the light of the Protestant Reformation, a little group of die-hard reformers landed on the shores of the New World. With them, the practice of reform through voluntarily living out biblical principles in the power of the Gospel was imprinted on the earliest DNA of what would become America.

The Great Experiment

When I was a schoolchild, tracing my hand to make a turkey craft for Thanksgiving, I picked up the common impression that the Pilgrims were a bunch of religious fuddy-duddies who dressed weird, were too dumb to grow corn, and whose greatest achievement was eating a meal with Indians that we were still commemorating yummily every

November. I might still have a similar impression of the Pilgrims if I hadn't gone on an international trip in 2011 to trace the real history of these people for a documentary called *Monumental*.[2]

The first stop on my trip was the little town of Scrooby in central England. The group later to be known as the Pilgrims, in the years around 1600, met in secret at a Scrooby manor house, using their children as lookouts to warn them if the authorities were coming to get them. At any time they could be arrested...or worse.

Why? What was so threatening about a bunch of Christians reading the Bible by candlelight and worshiping together?

I learned that the Pilgrims were a part of the Puritan movement, so named because they wanted to purify (reform) the Church of England. Except that some of the Puritans—the Separatists or Nonconformists—took it further, believing they should have full control of their own congregations. The Pilgrims were among these Separatists, not wanting to be subject to the monarch or high church officials in matters of faith and worship.

The Puritans, and especially the Separatists, paid a high price for their beliefs, with property confiscated, leaders thrown in jail, and even some executed. When persecution ratcheted up again around 1605, the Pilgrims began talking about how to get out of England. This is when they began their long pilgrimage to find a place where they could be free and let the light of the Gospel shine. This is also the point where we start to see how tough and determined these people really were. They just wouldn't give up!

Having left Scrooby for the south of England, I stood on the seashore at the place where the Pilgrims gathered to depart for the first location they hoped would become their new home—Holland.

In their original attempt to get to the Netherlands, the sea captain they had hired to transport them across the Channel sold them out to the local authorities. This Judas arranged for the Pilgrim men to be arrested and taken to jail, and he kept most of the Pilgrims' money and goods as the reward for his betrayal.

The men eventually got out of jail, and the group planned a second attempt to leave England. Only this time it was even more dangerous.

A storm of a magnitude not seen in many years struck just when the Pilgrims were planning to cross the English Channel for Holland once more. The women and children were on a raft that got stuck on a mudbank. Worse, the men were on board a little Dutch ship that headed into the North Sea at the mercy of winds that blew for two solid weeks. Many times, the ship seemed sure to go down, but the Pilgrims prayed, and when the sun finally came out, the ship, though battered, was still riding the waves. About a hundred ships are believed to have sunk in that storm, but by God's providence the Pilgrims' ship made it to Leiden, Holland, where the men were overjoyed some months later to be joined by their wives and children.

I walked the streets of Leiden and tried to imagine what it was like when the Pilgrims moved there around 1607. For a while it was a welcome haven, a place offering more religious freedom than most. But as the years passed, and for a variety of reasons, some of the Pilgrims came to believe Holland wasn't going to be a good place for them over the long run. Their thoughts began turning to the New World, which had recently begun to receive attention from the British as a likely site for colonization. A member of the group, William Bradford, recalled, "A great hope and inward zeal they had for the propagating and advancing the gospel of the kingdom of Christ in those remote parts of the world; yea, though they should be but even as stepping-stones unto others for the performing of so great a work."[3]

The first ship they chose to transport them to New England— the *Speedwell*—proved to be neither speedy nor well. It took on water before it got out of sight of England, and it had to be towed back to port. Soon after, 102 Pilgrims boarded a second ship, the *Mayflower*, and set sail in her for the west. I went aboard the full-scale replica of the *Mayflower*, now docked as a floating museum in Plymouth, Massachusetts, and it took no time at all to realize that the journey must have been horribly uncomfortable in this cramped ship, especially with the contrary winds the Pilgrims encountered.[4]

The journey lasted much longer than anticipated, but the delay gave them time to agree on a framework for their civil governance upon landing. Their pastor, John Robinson, who had stayed behind in Holland with the larger part of the congregation, had urged the Pilgrims in a letter to set up a government in New England, electing wise representatives who would make decisions with both God's ordinances and the common good in mind.[5] On board the ship, which contained both believers and nonbelievers ("saints and strangers"), the Pilgrims and the ship's crew members signed the Mayflower Compact, a simple constitution.[6]

What stands out to me most about the compact are the purposes its signers identified at the beginning: "for the Glory of God, and Advancement of the Christian Faith." Although this was a civil charter, there was no thought of creating a "secular" government on "secular" bases. The Pilgrims had Gospel purposes at the very heart of their project; therefore, the creation of the compact was their occasion to "solemnly and mutually, in the Presence of God and one another, covenant and combine ourselves together into a civil Body Politick, for our better Ordering and Preservation."

The Pilgrims' commitment to their vision would be swiftly and horrifically tested. It was nearly Christmas by the time they set foot on land, and they were far from prepared for the winter. The cold was brutal, forcing moms to sleep on their children to keep them warm—and sometimes the moms were not breathing by the time dawn appeared. Respiratory illness circulated throughout the group. At the lowest point, only six or seven of the Pilgrims were strong enough to walk, tending to the others and burying the dead. By March 1621, forty-seven of the Pilgrims who had made it across the ocean were dead.

With the improvement in weather by springtime, the captain was ready to return to England, expecting to take all the survivors with him. After all, this place had clearly proved inhospitable. The captain *asked* the Pilgrims to come with him. Then he *begged* them. *But not one of the Pilgrims agreed to go.* They still believed in that Mayflower Compact dream of the glory of God and the advancement of the Christian faith in this place.

This reminds me of the story of Gideon in the Bible, when God whittled his army down from thirty-two thousand, to ten thousand, and finally to three hundred men. This number was all it took for the Lord to engineer total victory over the invading Midianites (Judges 7). And likewise the Pilgrim colonists who clung to the rocky coast of New England, having been reduced to only about fifty, showed the Lord's greatness by their very littleness.

I walked the Plimoth Patuxet settlement—basically a cluster of simple houses and gardens enclosed within a wooden fence—and wondered how the Pilgrims could have dared to stay here rather than go back to England. I think they must have understood that throughout history God has always used a small group of people who are totally committed and all in. And they knew that if they kept their covenant with God and with one another, God would be faithful. This was the great experiment.

Bradford summarized, "Thus out of small beginnings greater things have been produced by His hand that made all things of nothing, and gives being to all things that are; and, as one small candle may light a thousand, so the light here kindled hath shone unto many."[7] In the same spirit, one of the Puritans who followed the Pilgrims to the New World said, "We must consider that we shall be as a city upon a hill. The eyes of all people are upon us."[8] The Pilgrims saw their little settlement on the edge of a vast and unknown continent as just that kind of city upon a hill shining the light of the Gospel for the whole world to see.

The American Covenant

The historian Marshall Foster appeared in the documentary *Monumental* and became a good friend and mentor of mine. His major book, *The American Covenant*, presents a view of America I had never encountered before, nor have most of us. According to Marshall, the way in which America was founded amounted to the forming of a covenant with God (a *covenant* being a type of sacred agreement or contract).

There are several covenants described in the Bible—the covenant of Moses, the covenant of David, the new covenant, and so on—and the American Covenant obviously isn't one of them, but it's possible to have covenants apart from the biblical context. For example, marriage is often described as a covenant. Today, America is typically seen as a "secular" country, but if you look into its origins, you find out that it was based in a covenant with one another in the presence of God.

Although not all the Founding Fathers and Mothers were devout or orthodox Christians, most were—and the rest had been heavily influenced by scriptural teaching. And so, starting with the Mayflower Compact's "for the Glory of God, and Advancement of the Christian Faith," many of America's earliest documents and public statements express submission to Almighty God. Consider these examples.

The Charter of Virginia (1606):

We, greatly commending, and graciously accepting of, their Desires for the Furtherance of so noble a Work, which may, by the Providence of Almighty God, hereafter tend to the Glory of his Divine Majesty, in propagating of Christian Religion to such People, as yet live in Darkness and miserable Ignorance of the true Knowledge and Worship of God, and may in time bring [such People], living in those parts, to human Civility, and to a settled and quiet Government.[9]

"The Declaration of the Causes and Necessity of Taking Up Arms" by the Continental Congress (1775):

With an humble confidence in the mercies of the supreme and impartial Judge and Ruler of the Universe, we most devoutly implore his divine goodness to protect us happily through this great conflict, to dispose our adversaries to reconciliation on reasonable terms, and thereby to relieve the empire from the calamities of civil war.[10]

The Declaration of Independence, signed July 4, 1776, is in the form of a covenant, an agreement among the people in the presence of God to establish a new nation. It concludes with a testimony stating that the revolutionaries' action was undertaken "with a firm reliance on the protection of divine Providence."

The US Constitution *does not* have any references to God in it. But in a way, it doesn't need to, because the whole thing is based on the biblical principles found in the Declaration of Independence. In other words, you cannot understand the Constitution if you don't understand the Declaration of Independence. Having come from a Europe that still believed in "the divine right of kings," James Madison and the other Framers put together a document investing power in the people themselves, leaving God as their only

King. Understanding the biblical doctrine of the innate sinfulness of humanity, the Framers also created a government with different levels and branches of government, a representative legislature, enumeration of powers, and a bill of rights, thus putting in place multiple checks and balances to prevent anyone's consolidating the absolute power that corrupts absolutely.

The Framers made a crucial assumption about a basis of faith in the American people if their document was going to be successful. President John Adams said, "Our Constitution was made only for a moral and religious People. It is wholly inadequate to the government of any other."[11]

Marshall Foster once listed principles of liberty derived from the Word of God and embedded in the Constitution and the American tradition. These included "civil equality, inalienable rights, the people's choice of their leaders, accountability of the public officials to the people and to God, justice in the courts with impartial juries, balance of powers with several branches of government, private property, prosperity resulting from a strong work ethic and faith, a stable economy backed by a hard currency, the centrality of the monogamous family, the sanctity of human life, education as a parental responsibility and social welfare through personal charity, not government largesse."[12] In other words, almost everything that makes America great.

Over the years, the people of America have created many public agreements saying that we will make laws intended to do the most good for the most people, and we'll do it with a clear conscience in the sight of God. Apart from official civil documents, Americans have also made many other kinds of covenants—personal covenants with God, family covenants, church covenants, and other covenants with one another in the presence of God. All these covenants are threads that, woven together, make up the fabric of the American

Covenant. And what a strong fabric it is! It's like Kevlar, the super-strong woven plastic fabric used in the bulletproof vest I wear when speaking in potentially hazardous settings. The American Covenant protects us from evils within and evils without.

America has been a greatly blessed nation, with such peace, freedom, and prosperity that to this day foreigners in their millions are desperate to get in. And certainly some of our good fortune has been due to such causes as the natural resources God placed within our borders. But the bigger reason—and the one that so often goes overlooked—is the godly basis on which our Founders established us. That is, because of the American Covenant.

The Bible not only tells about many times when the Israelites received or participated in establishing covenants with God at turning points in their history; it also tells about times when they *renewed* covenants. For example, after the Hebrews had occupied the Promised Land, Joshua renewed the covenant of his predecessor, Moses (Joshua 24:1–28). Though the promise of possessing the land had now been filled, that didn't mean the nation no longer needed to be obedient to God. Their future well-being in the "land of milk and honey" (*their* abundant natural resources) would depend on a continued commitment to the covenant. "The people said to Joshua, 'We will serve the Lord our God and obey him'" (verse 24).

In a way, this is what *Born to Be Brave* is: a call to renew the American Covenant. To pick up our historic vision of being a nation under God and carry that commitment boldly into a future full of unknowns and the presence of God.

Reform Yourself First

By this point, I might have you all fired up to want to begin a second American Revolution and bring liberty back. You might even be ready to take to the streets, to overthrow the powerful, to do almost anything to restore constitutional rights and get back to our Forefathers' values and principles.

If this is so, I admire your zeal, and I certainly don't want to squelch enthusiasm. But it's possible to overreact as well as underreact to the current cultural turmoil. So let me tell you what I always tell would-be revolutionaries: *before you go all 1776 to save the nation, first turn to Psalm 17:6.* This is the opposite of a call to grab your guns and head for the barricades. It's a humble plea for help.

> I call on you, my God, for you will answer me;
> turn your ear to me and hear my prayer.
> Show me the wonders of your great love,
> you who save by your right hand
> those who take refuge in you. (verses 6–7)

You see, if we want to pursue *not our own wants* but *God's agenda,* we've got to turn to Him and get right with Him, seeking His help and guidance.

If you have renewal in your own heart, it will change things, including your own motivations for wanting to bring change to the world. Instead of seeking social transformation because you're mad at things that have happened to you or because you believe you're so smart that you've figured everything out, you'll want to bring transformation God's way and in His timing because it's right and best for everybody.

It's great to be a reformer and not a reporter, but *reform yourself first.* Men and women with reformed hearts can reform their family. And then reformed families can reform their community. But it starts with humbling and examining ourselves.

I'll be saying more about this in a future chapter, but for now, please remember:

Don't just seek reformation. Be a reformation.

All In

I have a lot of respect for good reporters, ones who are working hard to discover the truth and share it fairly. Believe it or not, there are quite a few of them in the media! They're practicing true journalism, and good for them.

The kind of "reporting" I'm criticizing in this chapter is something very different: it's when any of us are over-quick to spread "news" about apparent problems in society without being involved in solutions. If all we're going to do is forward shocking social media posts to our friends, write flaming comments to a news article, or become that angry guy or girl who is always ready to spew forth about what's wrong with America—*but we aren't doing anything for positive change*—then we're not accomplishing anything.

So ask yourself, am I a reporter or a reformer? Too much reporting, in this sense, is actually a sign that the Left's strategy to make you irrelevant and ineffective is working. Defy them. Channel your emotions and energies in another way—toward finding a place where you can help to change the current social realities.

If you aren't interested in personally becoming a part of the brave-born reform movement, you might as well stop reading this book now. But I believe that isn't the case. I believe you want to *do* and not just *tell*. The Lord will get His work done no matter what, but I'm happy you're going to be a part of it, because contributing is always more meaningful and satisfying in the end than mere criticizing.

I hope it's been clear that in this chapter I've been speaking to you, whether you're a man or a woman, because I believe both sexes are equally responsible for helping in the reform of families and our nation. But next I'll specifically be talking about the sex that is most missing in action today. Get ready for it, bros.

CHAPTER 4

Arise, Warrior!

*If you think tough men are dangerous,
wait until you see what weak men are capable of.*

—JORDAN PETERSON

Why do so many men watch MMA matches? Why do they lose their minds over an NFL game? Why do they idolize basketball players or soccer stars? Or spend hours playing video games like *Call of Duty*? Or watch movies like *Rocky*, *Braveheart*, and *Gladiator* over and over again?

It's really not hard to understand. They're living vicariously through other men (even fictional men) who get to do bold, competitive, and consequential things. In doing this, men are finding an outlet for qualities that were built into them by their Creator.

Men and women have been called to be fruitful and increase in number and fill the earth and subdue it, ruling over the natural world. But specifically, just as God called the first man, Adam, to tend and look after the Garden of Eden, so men in every generation want to produce things and to guard and protect. As the generally stronger gender, we often want to take the lead in projects that require physical prowess. We tend to be assertive, competitive, and goal oriented.

I've got much more to say about the nature of men, but for now let me shift my line of questioning. Why are men today watching ball games and war movies, and killing bad guys in a virtual world, *when there are real enemies out there to contend with?* In particular, why are *men of faith* choosing to live vicariously, more likely to wear some athlete's jersey and watch TV than to put on the armor of God and go out to fight the powers of this dark world?

One reason is that the church's vision for men has shrunk down to something that is better suited to mice than men.

What do many churches say to their men? Isn't it stuff like the following? "Hey, guys, stop looking at porn. Try to be nicer to your wife, and stay out of trouble till the Rapture comes. By the way, could you set up the tables in the fellowship hall?" All that may be right and good as far as it goes, but it's *so* limited. Does any of it inspire men to unleash their inner braveheart—to extinguish evil with supernatural power and weapons, to advance the kingdom of God and of the good? Is it any wonder that so many men are bored and disengaged with church, leaving women to do most of the work while the men are on a couch in front of a screen?

Check out the Hall of Faith in Hebrews 11 and see if it resembles at all the puny vision that the present-day church holds out for its men.

Or would the apostle Paul, survivor of shipwreck, stoning, and imprisonment for the sake of his mission, recognize the small call of the present-day church to men?

Would Francis of Assisi, who crossed battle lines during one Crusade to preach the Gospel to Muslim leaders?

Would Patrick, who returned to the place where he'd been held as a captive and led the conversion of the entire nation of Ireland?

Would Martin Luther, who said, "Here I stand, I can do no other," when he challenged a corrupt church?

Today, within the family of faith, where is the call to conquer the forces of darkness? Why don't we challenge men to change the shape of society for Jesus? Why don't we expect them to take on big issues—like becoming the dominant leaders within the entertainment industry that shapes our culture, filling the seats of power in local and national governments to ensure good and just laws, advancing medical freedom and educational excellence, eradicating racism and child trafficking, and curing poverty, crime, and homelessness?

Men *want* these challenges. They want not just to do safe little church activities but to go out into the world and crush the heads of serpents. They want to do more than talk; they want to *act*. They want to take risks and test their bravery, like soldier recruits sent into battle. They'll respond, if given the opportunity and a little encouragement. Yet in our present-day culture the battle seems to be about whether they should even think of themselves as fighters.

Certainly there have been far too many times in history when cultures have undervalued women, and it's a deplorable mistake, but now we find ourselves at a different place. In the Woke West, many of the influential in society are not just trying to raise the status of women but are doing it at the expense of men. They deride masculinity itself. The unfortunate possessors of a Y chromosome need to be reprogrammed with a new kind of "manliness," one that looks a lot like the old womanliness.

The truth here? Being male is *not* a negative instinct to be tamed, an adverse socialization to be unlearned, or a pathology to be medicated. While there *is* such a thing as toxic masculinity, producing behaviors like sexual assault, domestic violence, pornography use, and bullying, masculinity itself is not toxic. These things happen when men neglect the sacred call of good and godly manhood. Biblical masculinity is the opposite of these cowardly behaviors.

One thing that makes me mad about the feminization of men is that in many cases the family of faith has embraced it. Perhaps this trend seems gentler, "nicer," more Christlike. Anything resembling the warlike or aggressive can't be Christian, can it? That's what many Christians think. But I don't believe God is happy that a human gender He created in a specific way is being unnaturally forced to look like the other gender. His image in humanity is reduced to half its glory if it's only feminine.

Women and men share the call to reform society for Christ equally, but if we're looking for a recovery of second-birth bravery in this day, we'd better recognize the special need for the church to help men start playing their roles in the world. Men represent a vast untapped aquifer for bravery. I'd go so far as to say that, if men *don't* step up, the new bravery movement simply will not have enough juice to push along a major spiritual comeback in our day.

If you're one of the men of faith who have been effectively neutered and neutralized, causing you to spend too much time diverting your masculine qualities into substitutes like sports and gaming, Jesus is calling out to you, "Arise! Turn off the football game and get up from your couch. Put down your video game controller and arise! Stop living vicariously and start living victoriously."

The Good Monster

If you're steeped in the modern-day scorn for masculinity, get ready for a shocker. Canadian psychologist Jordan Peterson says men need to restore their inner *monster*.

Everyone says you shouldn't do anyone any harm. You should sheath your competitive instinct. You shouldn't try to win. You don't want to be too aggressive. You don't want to be too assertive. You want to take a back seat and all of that.

Wrong.

You should be a monster, an absolute monster...and then you should learn how to control it.[1]

Peterson looked into the meaning of the New Testament word *meek*, as in *the meek will inherit the earth*. He says, "It means something more like *Those who have swords and know how to use them, but keep them sheathed, will inherit the world*." My favorite image representing the Greek word for *meek* is a massive warhorse that charges into battle with just a nudge from its rider, doing only what it is commanded to do. Meek means being totally compliant to the command of God regardless of the personal cost to us. Christian gentleness is not powerlessness but immense power under wise control and direction.

What good is self-learned weakness in a man? That's anti-bravery. Without men—*strong* men—to partner with women, the culture will likely never be remade. The modern emasculated male is of little use to anybody. Peterson goes on:

If you're harmless, you're not virtuous. You're just harmless. You're like a rabbit. A rabbit isn't virtuous. It can't do anything except get eaten.

If you're a monster and you don't act monstrously, then you're virtuous. But you also have to be a monster.

The discernment to know when to act in power, and the self-control to hold in our power until the right time has come, are crucial. We should remember the example of Peter, who should have kept his sword at his side instead of slicing off the servant Malchus's ear (John 18:10–11). But at the same time, discernment and self-control are no good unless we embody a real threat to evil.

Demons were terrified when they encountered Jesus. Does anyone sense danger to their unrighteous causes when they see us coming? Narnia's Aslan, representing Christ, was not a tame lion— he was good, but he wasn't safe. Neither should we be tame or entirely safe. We're submitted to God, and we seek to be self-controlled, but to the forces of evil we must be dangerous. We must stop merely reacting and instead take the offensive in social change so that others are reacting to us.

Instead of conquering manhood, why don't we encourage men to go out and conquer evil? I think men want to be beasts who have such a principled approach to life that they can direct their strength and their manhood in a way that is consistent with the fruit of the Spirit, promotes the good, protects their wives and children, if they have them, and furthers the kingdom of God.

The Rabbi Is a General

If Jordan Peterson is right, there should be a monster inside a man. If you don't like *monster*, substitute *warrior*. If you don't like *warrior*, I can't help you, because Scripture uses that metaphor many times.

Let me show you the other Jesus.

In His first coming, Jesus was a rabbi in sandals. He led a group of rather hapless ministry students in an outdoor school. He never took up arms in battle, nor organized a coup against the Roman occupiers, nor tried to take the Jewish religious system into His own hands. When tossed an opportunity to instigate a tax revolt against the emperor, He turned it into a lesson in faithfulness to God (Mark 12:13–17). When He was taken into custody, His captors mocked His kingliness by outfitting Him with a fake scepter, a fake royal robe, and a crown of thorns, because to them the claim that He was a king seemed a joke. Having humbly come to earth as a baby, He ended up even more humbly, submitting Himself to the cruel death reserved for criminals (Philippians 2:5–8).

If you're not familiar with the Scriptures, it might seem that Jesus more or less fits the mold of the modern feminized man: nonviolent, nonthreatening, preaching love and forgiveness. According to some popular artists' representations, He often *looks* a little transgendered. But even during His earthly ministry He exemplified an extraordinary masculine strength that could at times be "triggering." Attempts by the Jewish leaders to trap Him left Him unperturbed, and He didn't hesitate to call them hypocrites in graphic terms. When the time came to give up His life, "Jesus resolutely set out for Jerusalem" (Luke 9:51), or as one prophet foresaw this pivotal moment, He "set his face like flint" (see Isaiah 50:7)—*that's* determination in the face of certain harm. When Jesus repaired Peter's impulsive violence to Malchus's ear, He said, "Do you think I cannot call on my Father, and he will at once put at my disposal more than twelve legions of angels?" (Matthew 26:53). In Peterson's terms, He was a monster under control. He was Meek Jesus, but He was also Brave Jesus.

One day the fully faceted awesomeness of this Brave Jesus will be unveiled for all to see. Just as a Marvel or DC Comics superhero identity can be hidden within a seemingly ordinary person, there's more to Jesus than some perceive. The sacrificial Lamb is also the Lion of the Tribe of Judah.

At His second coming, Jesus is a warrior (Revelation 19:11–18). He is riding a white horse and going out to make war against His enemies, with an angelic army arrayed behind Him. Out of His mouth comes a sword. His robe is already dripping with blood, and more blood is going to flow like the juice of grapes crushed in the "winepress of the fury of the wrath of God Almighty." His title is emblazoned on His robe like a name on a football jersey: KING OF KINGS AND LORD OF LORDS. The bodies of His foes are about to become a feast for carrion-eating birds.

I almost feel like I should apologize for the violence of this imagery. But every bit of it is straight from Scripture!

The real Jesus—the one we tend to forget—is a warrior of warriors. He is the ultimate archetype for every hero and superhero in history. A man today who wants to be known for flinty determination, who wants to be a monster under control, directing his God-given strength toward epic causes that reverberate in Heaven and earth, will follow the lead of General Jesus. He'll be a lion for the Lion of the Tribe of Judah. Anything less comes with its own risk.

When Dominion Becomes Domination

All the evil in the world traces back to a man failing to honor God through protecting and preserving.

As we've seen, the human race in general was given the commands to "rule over...the earth" and to "fill the earth and subdue it" (Genesis 1:26, 28). More specifically, the first human being, Adam, was put in the garden of Eden with instructions "to work it and keep it" (2:15, ESV). The Hebrew term translated "work it" means to cultivate the garden. The term translated "keep it" means to protect it. So Adam was supposed to be both a *gardener* and a *guard* for Eden.

God also gave Adam a wife, who it was his responsibility to take care of (Ephesians 5:28–30). So when a serpent came slithering up to Eve and started encouraging disobedience to God, Adam should have said, "Stop right there! Get behind me, Satan." But as we know, he did not.

The result was that Adam and Eve were cursed and found themselves evicted from the garden. The same word for "keep it" from

Genesis 2:15 is used in Genesis 3:24 of the angel set to "guard" the tree of life after the couple's departure; so ironically, and sadly, the man instructed to *keep* the garden ended up being *kept out* of it. And because Adam had a special position in covenant with God, all his descendants have been affected by sin ever since, like him broken and suffering, separated from a blessed relationship with God.

After the Fall, the "subduing," or dominion, that God commanded of the human race all too often got twisted. Instead of taking dominion over the land, people started taking dominion over other people. By just the second generation, Cain killed Abel. And the problem grew from there. Rather than creating a culture that would have reflected the beauties and truths of God, and done good for all people, early humans did the opposite and reached a point where it was all evil all the time.

The Flood cleared the slate for a new starting point, but the whole history of the world since Noah has been stained by dominion that's been turned into domination: the strong enslaving the weak, men tyrannizing women, governments oppressing citizens, the rich taking advantage of the poor, and so on. This domineering tendency has always been a brake on the speed of the progress of human flourishing. And let's be truthful: men have been more responsible for this domination than women.

There's a reason the "bad guys" in the world's tales are almost always literal *guys*—it's art mimicking life.

History's dictators, psychopaths, and terrorists have overwhelmingly been male.

Criminology experts tell us that gender is the single best predictor of criminal behavior, with men committing more crimes than women, and that this has been true throughout history, in all societies, and in nearly every crime category.

Does all this mean that the feminizers of men are right? That masculinity is so inherently harmful that we ought to be canceling it, like we're canceling so many other things these days?

Something very different is true. The solution isn't to take manhood away from men but to restore them to *proper* manhood— strength under control, and competitiveness directed not at building's one's own empires but at doing the will of God. In fact, society's problems will *never* be fixed until this occurs, because men who fail to act honorably and courageously when they should do so leave a vacuum for evil to enter. Like Adam, they are to be guards in this world, blocking the way of evil, including the evil that other men do.

I would argue that Adam's failure to guard the garden and protect his wife was the first sin. It is true that Eve was the first to be deceived, but Adam was the first to sin (Romans 5:12). And male passivity remains an ever-present temptation today. Thank God for Jesus, the second Adam, who reversed the first Adam's failure in the Garden of Eden. On the night when Jesus was praying in the Garden of Gethsemane, Judas (after Satan had entered into him, as we see in Luke 22:3) slithered in like a serpent along with a detachment of soldiers. Jesus had His "bride" (represented by the faithful disciples) with Him, and He guarded this bride successfully by telling the soldiers to leave the disciples alone and surrendering Himself into custody—He went to the cross to do battle with the forces of darkness—He "gave himself up for her," as a good husband should (Ephesians 5:25) and there He crushed the serpent's head.

Jesus offers us the greatest example of manliness. As He has dominion over us, He will train us to have dominion over ourselves, and we will then be equipped to take a proper dominion over the earth.

The journey to true masculine bravery is one that each man must take for himself, step by step. One of my favorite recent examples comes from my friend Jonathan Isaac.

He Stood

Prior to the start of the July 31, 2020, basketball game between the Brooklyn Nets and the Orlando Magic, the team members sat or knelt as the US national anthem played inside the NBA Bubble. NFL quarterback Colin Kaepernick had started a trend four years earlier, and by this time, refusing to stand during the anthem was becoming expected within many professional sports. On this night—just two months after the tragic death of George Floyd—the basketball players were also wearing Black Lives Matter T-shirts. To those participating in these trends, they were protesting racial injustice and police brutality. To others, it looked like showing disrespect to the flag, with some virtue signaling thrown in.

But this game was notable because one player bucked the trend.

Magic power forward Jonathan Isaac stood out under the stadium lights, not just because he was six foot ten with long hair that made him seem even taller, but because he was on his feet, head bowed, and wearing a white team jersey. Isaac had suffered from anxiety and insecurity for years—he had been more detached from his circumstances than he'd wanted and had often stayed in the shadows—but on this occasion he found the courage to stand alone, despite knowing he would take heat for what he did.

Later he was asked why he made this bold choice.

"I don't think that kneeling or putting on a T-shirt for me personally is the answer," Isaac said. "I feel like Black lives are supported through the gospel, all lives are supported through the gospel. And we all have things that we do wrong and sometimes it gets to a place of pointing fingers about [whose] wrong is worse."

He went on to say that humbling ourselves and repenting "would help bring us closer together and get past anything that's on the surface that doesn't really deal with the hearts of men and women."[2]

In the years since then, throughout a professional basketball career marked by plenty of highs and lows, injuries and recovery, Isaac has continued to take a bold approach to his beliefs.

Responding to the way that major apparel brands have adopted divisive agendas, Isaac started his own athletic-wear brand in 2023. It is called UNITUS, and Isaac hopes it will unite people rather than divide them. "UNITUS is a community of people rallied around faith, family, freedom, and the pursuit of true greatness."[3]

He also demonstrates the loving and humble, yet firm, attitude that we should have as we go about being brave. "It's not about hating anybody," he says. "It's not about talking down to other people. It's saying, 'This is what I believe. I respect what you believe, and I will discourse with you. I'll talk with you about why I believe what I believe. And at the end of the day, it may be that we agree to disagree, but I will not stop standing up for what I believe in.'"[4]

If men today want to be like Isaac and have the bravery to stand up for what we believe in, we may just need a push. Some en-*courage*-ment.

Be Strong and Courageous

We may look back at towering Christian figures of our own national past and feel inferior, wondering if, like them, we could possibly have what it takes to achieve revolutionary change for the good. But just imagine how Joshua felt when he took Moses's place (Joshua 1). For forty years Moses led the people of Israel through the Exodus and the Red Sea, law giving, tabernacle building, rebellions, and wars, right up to the border of the Promised Land. And *those* were the shoes Joshua was supposed to fill?

To raise the stakes even higher, Joshua was not taking over the national leadership in a mere maintenance role, like a newly elected president coming into office in a time of peace and prosperity. No.

Joshua was being given the responsibility of accomplishing what the forty-year Exodus had been leading up to all along: taking the land of Canaan so that the Hebrews could settle in it permanently. Over there, on the other side of that river, it lay—a land of great promise and equal peril.

No doubt Joshua was a brave man, probably braver than most others. But when God said now was the time to launch the invasion, Joshua knew what it meant. He would give orders that would set armies in motion; thousands of people would suffer and die. The options were victory or an unprecedented setback for his people. Surely Joshua felt a tremendous weight from the work he was expected to do.

So God dealt with the need inside Joshua's heart. "Be strong and courageous," the Lord said, "because you will lead these people to inherit the land I swore to their ancestors to give them" (Joshua 1:6). Twice more, so Joshua couldn't possibly mistake His words, the Lord said it: *Be strong and courageous!*

God will never tell us to fear another person. We'd better have a sober respect for the One who has authority over our destiny in this life and the next (Matthew 10:28), but mere human opponents?

Fear not.

Be strong and courageous.

Be brave.

Attaching a guarantee to his encouragement to Joshua, God promised His own presence. "I will be with you; I will never leave you nor forsake you" (Joshua 1:5). This same reassurance reappears thirteen more times throughout the book of Joshua.[5] The promise of God's presence isn't just a nice add-on; Joshua's courage would be *produced* by his connection with God. One commentator on this chapter of the Bible wrote, "Joshua is not told to grit his teeth and screw up his courage on his own; he is to be strong only because

69

BORN TO BE BRAVE

Yahweh is with him (v. 9) and not because Yahweh prefers leaders who are positive thinkers."[6]

With this perspective in mind, Jesus's promise at the end of His great commission to His followers takes on some extra meaning. "Surely I am with you always, to the very end of the age" (Matthew 28:20). For followers of Jesus, *our* courage is never about mere positive thinking either. Living out our second-birth courage is not about being determined and trying hard; it's about relying on God's presence with us. We're fruitful as we abide in Jesus.

Men today are capable of rising to the tasks before us, if we are challenged and encouraged. I believe God is saying to men today, "Be strong and courageous." Pastors should be telling the men in their congregations the same thing. Wives should be saying to their husbands and guy friends should be saying to each other, "Be strong and courageous!"

Any guy sitting on a couch with a remote in his hand can become a godly warrior if he is strong and courageous and backed by other warriors who are strong and courageous too.

Red Truck Men

My friend Steve Thomas was at a crisis point in his life, feeling lonely and spiritually hurting, when he invited a few male friends to join him for breakfast and some Scripture reading once a week. Evidently there were a lot of disconnected, disengaged men out there, hungry to find their way together, because other guys heard about the morning meetings and asked if they could join. At first a few. Then dozens. Steve realized God was doing something here, and eventually he created an organization to accommodate it.

Steve calls his ministry Red Truck Men, since one experience that practically all males shared when they were boys—and often still share in adulthood—is a love of big red fire trucks. "When you hear a siren and watch a fire engine rush to a burning building," says Steve, "it elicits a feeling of respect and honor. The men on board that Red Truck are heroes. Selfless men whose profession is dedicated to responding to crisis and promoting a message of hope." Red Truck Men "desires to unite a band of brothers who build significant bonds of friendship as they serve their God, family and community with honor and humility."[7]

Now a couple thousand men are getting together in groups across the Carolinas, with more groups being added all the time. Red Truck Men owns a small fleet of red pickup trucks, the kind that look like a fire chief might own, and out of those trucks come the makings for the best breakfast that I, for one, have ever had. Sitting around a firepit, the men enjoy biscuits and gravy, and eggs, and bacon, and coffee, and whatever else they could wish for. Afterward, they open up the leather-bound Bibles that Red Truck Men provides, and they read some Scripture and discuss it, often getting into dangerous territory about topics like God, marriage, family, career, country, money, politics, and social contagions. When they're not having these conversations, the men do fun activities together, like hatchet throwing, skeet shooting, and sport fishing. They also organize in groups to work on service projects, like repair and landscaping for others who are in need.

With Red Truck Men, the participants are not being turned into a bunch of mice but instead are encouraged to grow into the kind of men God made them to be—servant warriors.

"We're not going to change our country by criticizing the politicians," Steve says. "We can only change our country by changing ourselves. The problem is, we can't change ourselves if we aren't working *together* on it. And that's what Red Truck Men does."

Not every man needs a red truck or smoky outdoor breakfast to settle comfortably into his masculinity and find his mission, but every man could use some friend, some mentor, some tribe, some band of brothers to help him become a hero of the faith—a "firefighter" rushing in, siren wailing, toward whatever inferno has broken out in society.

The Glorious Partnership

I've been trying to restore a lost perspective on the role of men in reforming the world's broken structures, but before I go any further, I want to be *very* clear that this does not imply the inferiority of women in any way. Women share equally in the image of God with men, and they have equal worth and dignity. Redeemed women, like redeemed men, are born to be brave, and their contribution is just as much needed for the anticipated cultural comeback. It has always been this way.

While men may feature in the stories of the Bible more often than women, God has left us indications from every era of biblical history that He loves women and strategically uses them in His plans. The story of the patriarchs who founded the nation of Israel would be unimaginable without the contributions made by their wives, Sarah, Rebekah, and Rachel. For example, it was Rebekah, not Isaac, who bravely initiated a plan for their son Jacob (Israel) to receive the family birthright, thus becoming the heir of God's promises in place of his twin, Esau. Jochebed and Miriam, Moses's mother and sister, bravely saved the future deliverer from murder when he was a baby. Rahab bravely hid the Hebrew spies in Jericho and helped them fulfill God's plan even against the interests of her own people. Deborah was a national leader and was the person to whom her general, Barak, looked for courage. It was Jael who killed the general that Barak was afraid to face. Ruth bravely stuck with her Hebrew mother-in-law, Naomi, in moving to Bethlehem. Hannah bravely trusted for a son, and later gave up her boy, Samuel, for training as a prophet. Jehosheba bravely rescued her infant nephew, the future king Joash, from death. Esther was so brave that I'm going to give her a featured story of her own in a future chapter. Mary of Nazareth bravely accepted the mission of giving birth to the Messiah, then endured the pain of watching Him undergo crucifixion. Mary Magdalene bravely followed Jesus through both popularity and persecution and was among the first to see Him resurrected.

Jesus was distinctly pro-female, mixing with women in society much more naturally than Jewish men of His day normally did, as in His encounter with the woman at the well (John 4) and in His friendship with Martha and Mary (Luke 10:38–42). Without the "women's auxiliary" (Luke 8:1–3), it's unclear how Jesus and the Twelve would have managed their practical affairs. Jesus's chief theologian, Paul, worked alongside many respected female Christians, including Priscilla, Phoebe, and Lydia. Paul made clear that the male-female distinction, while real, makes no difference when it comes to having unity with Christ (Galatians 3:28).

My wife of more than thirty years, Chelsea, has already provided so much sacrificial selflessness, boldness, and courage that, whatever I do, it will never be enough to catch up to her. Rewatch those episodes from the later seasons of *Growing Pains* where she plays Mike Seaver's girlfriend, and you'll see how stunning and talented she was, and yet it was not long after then that she gave up her modeling and acting career to take on me and eventually the six children we would raise together. I was always an involved dad, but Chelsea had the critical place in the education and the moral and spiritual molding of our kids, turning Deuteronomy 6 into the operating procedure of the Cam fam. Now young adults, the next generation has not turned from the way in which their mother and father trained them. Chelsea's maiden name was Noble, and I want to borrow Proverbs 31:29

and say this to her: "Many women do noble things, but you surpass them all."

I look at Chelsea and I know why women have been indispensable in advancing Christian faith and practice to this point in history. In this chapter I'm focusing on men because they are currently facing additional headwinds in a society where, somehow, it's fine for a biological female to choose masculinity, but if a man tries to live out his masculinity, he must be stripped and stopped. Men who insist on behaving with true masculinity—strong yet controlled and submitted to God—can raise their heads and take their proper place beside women in reforming the nation. Unless I'm mistaken, most women want them to.

That Guy

Recently I gave a message at a church on the same topic as this book—having the bravery to live out our faith and to work to transform society around biblical truth. In this message, I emphasized the particular problem we have in the church with men who are missing from the spiritual action.

Afterward, a guy who looked like he was about fifty-five came up to me. He had tears in his eyes, and he said, "I'm that guy. I've been that guy for the last fifteen years.

"I was in the army. I know what it means to stand for principle and fight for what's right. But I've become disillusioned. I've become jaded. I feel bitter. It seems like there's nothing I can do to change anything. And so I'm that guy that sits on the couch, trying to stay focused on a game, or maybe watching the news, and I can't seem to stop complaining and cursing the people that are doing all these bad things to our country.

"Kirk, you gave me hope that we can actually turn things around. I'm in. I'm ready to get up off the couch. What do I do?"

By this time, I had tears in my eyes too. It wasn't my speaking but the strong call of the Gospel to men (as well as women) that had called to the warrior inside this vet, "Arise!"

His question was the right one. *What do I do?* That's what the rest of this book is about.

CHAPTER 5

A Vision of Victory

*The most serious error in much of the current prophetic teaching is
the claim that the future of Christianity is to be read not in terms of
revival and victory, but of growing impotence and apostasy.*

—OSWALD T. ALLIS

Before Ronald Reagan came along, America's approach to the Cold
War was détente, a gradual relaxing of tensions and shrinking of
arsenals. It was a policy that guaranteed a lengthy stalemate, but at
least it lowered the risks, right?

Ronald Reagan had a different idea about the Cold War. He
wanted to *win* it.[1]

People called him naive, ignorant, even dangerous. But he had a
plan that involved magnifying America's military advantage to the
point that people living under Soviet communism would see how
inferior their system was and become restless with Kremlin lies and
Kremlin rule.

The amazing thing is, it worked. Not long after Reagan left the
White House, Soviet communism collapsed, and millions of people

in Europe and Asia suddenly found themselves enjoying a freedom they had never believed they would see in their lifetimes. Simultaneously, America had the Cold War monkey lifted off her back.

The miracle would never have played out like that if a president and a small minority of others weren't convinced it was possible.

When the Vikings were sweeping through ninth-century Britain, most Britons had given up hope of freedom. But one man—Alfred of Wessex—believed it was still possible to win.

The tiny band of Pilgrims—through arrest, betrayal, poverty, storms, illness, and starvation—somehow sustained their belief that God would give them a home where they could form a faithful community that would shine a light for the world.

As the family of faith, in the middle of a major cultural setback, we can learn from others who have been in similar spots. To succeed in bringing hope, liberty, and truth to our world today, there's one indispensable thing we need first: a belief in our hearts that it can come to pass. Strategy's important too. But first the belief.

A vision of victory transforms bravery from a short burst of emotion into a long-lasting, sustainable character trait. It takes us out of our isolation and puts us in the community of those who share the same vision we do. It gets us moving, because it defines a trajectory toward a goal. It gives us a purpose to live for that's bigger than ourselves, while simultaneously humbling us, because the victory isn't ours—it's God's.

David and Goliath and the Giant

Way too many Christians today have conceded defeat. They're thinking small because they're feeling small. I hear a lot of talk that boils down to this: "Look at Big Government. Look at Big Business. Look at Big Tech. They're too much for us." Or maybe people see a biased media-entertainment-academic-medical-political complex, and they view it as a network of such immense power and reach that we can never escape its control. Or an unfavorable majority in elected offices appears insurmountable.

Reminds me of the time when Moses sent twelve men on a reconnaissance mission of the land of Canaan before launching an invasion that God had called for (Numbers 13:1–33). Afterward, most of the men agreed that the challenge was too great: "Oh, you wouldn't believe how strong these people are, how impenetrable the walls around their cities are. We even saw a bunch of big, scary giants. We can't attack the Canaanites." One of the men, Caleb, remembered some words Moses had spoken earlier: "You may say to yourselves, 'These nations are stronger than we are. How can we drive them out?' But do not be afraid of them; remember well what the Lord your God did to Pharaoh and to all Egypt" (Deuteronomy 7:17–18). Caleb made an impassioned plea that the nation should go ahead with the invasion. Nevertheless, on this occasion the defeatists were in the majority and so the occupation of the Promised Land was put off for a generation.

The same pattern started to repeat itself a few centuries later when the Israelite army was encamped on the hills across from the Philistine army (1 Samuel 17). The Philistines cleverly put forward a towering, intimidating champion named Goliath to fight for them. And sure enough, none of the Israelites were willing to go up against this towering specimen of a man. The conflict remained at a standstill until a boy named David had the vision that Goliath was defeatable. Stone meets forehead. After that, the whole Israelite army was ready to attack.

The fact is that some people will always grasp a vision of victory before others do. They remember who they are and whose they are. They lock into the mission and seek to honor their Master. Bravery wells up within them, and the image of winning appears ahead of them. From this minority spreads the hope of victory to the majority. The twice-born brave are the vanguard of the army, the yeast in the dough, the catalyst to the reactant. *You* could be an early adopter of bravery in our day.

And if you are, you won't have to worry about whether your newborn confidence is just bravado or self-delusion. Because you see, the real giant in the story of David and Goliath wasn't who we usually think it was. Goliath was big, but David knew God was infinitely bigger. David cried out to the Philistines, "The battle is the Lord's, and he will give all of you into our hands" (verse 47).

Big Tech, Big Government, Big Whatever is always going to be minuscule next to our Big God. Instead of conceding defeat, let's claim victory in His name.

I know.... Easy to say, hard to achieve.

Let me give you two major reasons why Christians in our day are defeatist: either it's baked into their end-times theology, or they've swallowed the lie that the culture has drifted too far for recovery. See if you recognize any of your own thinking in the descriptions I'm about to give.

Leaving Pessimism Behind

When I travel, I talk to a lot of Christians about the state of the world we live in today. Roughly the same litany of issues tends to come up: the normalization of immorality, lawlessness on the streets, threats from China and Russia, conflict in the Middle East, and so on.

Then I ask people what they think our response should be as Christians.

Many times, this is what I hear: "Hey, what do you expect? These are the end times. The Bible says things are just going to get darker. But at least Jesus is coming back soon and we'll go to Heaven. We need to save all the souls we can before then."

I'll reply, "We definitely need to spread the good news of salvation. But don't you think we should *also* try to bring a godly perspective to bear on society, try to correct errors in the culture?"

"Yes, of course, but it's also important not to have any false hopes. The truth is, we don't win down here. We lose."

To them, trying to win the culture and fundamentally transform our institutions to conform to the Word of God makes as much sense as polishing the brass on a sinking ship. This is the perspective that their pastor teaches. Or perhaps this is an idea that was left behind in their mind from a book, or maybe from a movie. But I wonder if they also sort of *want* to believe it.

For many, there can be excitement built into the apparently apocalyptic nature of what's happening today. This dystopian universe that seems to be materializing in front of our eyes makes us think, *Wow, we could be the terminal generation, the one that sees the return of Christ in our lifetime. How exciting!* It's a sensational and alluring way to think.

The passivity of pessimism is also tempting because it appeals to our natural human tendency to take the easy road. Now, I'm *not* saying that people who believe this way are consciously deciding to be lazy. In fact, I have some friends who have bought into this way of thinking who are working harder to change culture and represent God in the public square than most other Christians I know. But they are the exception. Subconsciously, the mental paradigm of an inevitable doomsday can be appealing to avoid the hard work of redeeming our culture—of uprooting evil and rebuilding our society. I'm talking about hard work like raising a family and rearing children in the nurture and instruction of the Lord, carrying out evangelism and discipleship, sacrificing your evenings and weekends to impact local schools and your community, and donating your hard-earned savings to help your church lift up the poor and needy. It's way easier to say, "Let's have another Bible study on Revelation!"

I don't want to judge people's motives. I don't even want to rate end-time theologies here. What I do want to do is help us all think about how our beliefs about the end times are affecting *how we choose to live.*

If our view of biblical prophecy makes us believe that things are only going to get worse, then it becomes self-fulfilling prophecy. Christians will do little to improve things, so of course they do get worse. Take away the salt and the light from society, and the world gets rotted and dark for everybody.

On the other hand, if we focus on the faithfulness, power, and victory of our Savior (see Deuteronomy 31:8; Isaiah 9:6–7; Matthew 28:18–20; John 12:31–32; Revelation 17:14; 19:16), then regardless of where this generation may fit in the historical timetable, we have more than ample reason to believe that a blessed future here on earth is possible.

Just in the last few decades that I've been a believer, I've heard of several preachers who have falsely prophesied that the end was about to come at some specific date…which then passed. Jesus said His disciples wouldn't know the day or hour (Matthew 24:36), but if we were to reason from many of the sermons preached today, our culture has gotten so bad and the prophetic signs are allegedly aligning so quickly that we should expect D-day and the Rapture to be here by Tuesday! Why don't we ditch the pessimistic, escapist, defeatist mindset and adopt Jesus's own confident and victorious prayer as our guiding mandate: "Lord, use my life so that your kingdom may come and your will be done on earth as it is in Heaven."

Some people have been predicting the end of earthly history since Christ went to Heaven; others have been busy bringing Heaven to earth by doing what Jesus told them to do. What's your choice? I say, go ahead and polish that brass, and while you're at it, swab the deck, scrape the hull, stoke the coals, grab the wheel—full steam ahead! This ship is going forward, not down.

Unless you're still not sure because you've got another reason for being negative and discouraged about the Christian influence upon the culture....

Crossing the Line

I wonder what would happen if God came to me, like He came to Moses, Isaiah, Jeremiah, Mary, Paul, and many others, with a specific call to do something great for Him in this time. If I believed the pessimistic lying propaganda of our day, I doubt I'd say with the eagerness of Isaiah, "Here am I! Send me!" (Isaiah 6:8). Nor the humble submission of Mary, "I am the Lord's servant. May it be to me as you have said" (Luke 1:38). Instead, I might respond like this: "Um, sorry, Lord. I really appreciate your confidence in me, but it just isn't going to be possible to change anything. Haven't you heard? Us Christians are in a shrinking minority, and the power has shifted to others who don't like us. We pretty much need to stay in our own churchy environment, or it can get really bad for us."

And God would say, "Huh?"

It's standard these days to refer to America as "post-Christian." And I get it. The percentage of Americans who identify as Christian—about 90 percent when I was born in 1970—has dropped to 63 percent and seems headed lower.[2] We can no longer assume people have familiarity with the Bible, find Jesus to be special, or want society to be organized along biblical principles, if they even have a conception of what those might be. Many of the loudest voices in society seem to belong to non-Christians and anti-Christians. If we express our faith publicly today, there's a good chance we'll be misunderstood, misrepresented, and maybe even persecuted.

Things have changed, for sure. That's why the message of *Born to Be Brave* is so urgent and important to me. We need to see the reality clearly.

And yet the facts are one thing, and the conclusions we draw from them are another. Agreeing with the perspective of "post-Christianity" plays into the hands of Christ's opponents, who want to create the impression that Christianity has already lost and is well on its way to the trash dumpster of history. More importantly, when we adopt a post-Christian mindset, we lower our own expectations and narrow the range within which we seek to have a powerful influence.

While others are saying we've crossed some sort of invisible line from being a Christian nation to being a post-Christian one, let me tell you, *the only line that really matters is the one that Jesus crossed when He passed from death to life.*

The subject of eschatology is famously murky, leading to several incompatible views all put forward by people who love the Lord and believe the Bible. So maybe it's not so surprising that end-time interpretations have caused some to become pessimistic and passive while others remain hopeful and active on behalf of this world. But for those of us who believe in the faithfulness of God and His Word, there should be no disagreement at all about Jesus's victory over death and the devil and His power to transform hearts, homes, and nations.

Sometime, in Heaven, the Father gave the Son a mission to redeem sinful humanity. Unlike many of us who are too timid to do what God asks of us, Jesus freely accepted His mission. And what was His goal? "The reason the Son of God appeared was to destroy the devil's work" (1 John 3:8). By the time Jesus gave up His life, He knew He had fulfilled His earthly purpose and could declare, "It is finished" (John 19:30). The Resurrection verified His victory and sealed the fate of the devil.

Christ now reigns in Heaven at the right hand of the Father. All authority in Heaven and on earth belongs to Him. Meanwhile, here on earth He has entrusted His influence to us, His followers, as we continue to preach the good news and disciple entire nations, baptizing them and teaching them to obey all that Christ has commanded.

Who shall separate us from the love of Christ? Shall Supreme Court decisions, or loudmouth celebrities with their anti-Christian bias, or a graph of religious affiliation that isn't looking good for us, or an unbiblical form of morality enshrined in law? No, in all these things we are more than conquerors through Him who loved us.

The spirit of the Antichrist may be abroad in the land (it always has been!), and yet the one who is in us is *still* greater than the one who is in the world (1 John 4:1–6).

Sometimes when my fellow believers are getting grim, and that feeling's starting to seep into my own spirit, I like to think about how God sits on His throne in the heavens and laughs at nations that think they can overcome God's people (Psalm 2:1–6). It's ludicrous to presume Almighty God is any less in control, any less triumphant than He has ever been. We should react the same as He does to the silly assumptions of "post-Christianity": we should laugh!

We have got to have the mindset not that we are fighting *for* victory but that we are fighting *from* victory. Jesus has already won at the Crucifixion and at the Resurrection. We need to now operate according to what Christ has done and do what He's told us to do, and then we will begin to see the working out of what He has secured for us. "Of the increase of his government and peace," Isaiah says, "there will be no end" (Isaiah 9:7).

Now is not the time to raise the white flag, because if you are a Christian, it is *never* the right time to surrender. Remember Elisha's encouraging words to his servant in 2 Kings 6:16: "Don't be afraid.

Those who are with us are more than those who are with them." If we resist the indoctrination that somehow our enemies are too strong, that defeat is inevitable, that our best days are behind us and America has passed the time when her culture can be transformed, then we can begin to have hope...optimism...courage!

We might be amazed at what can happen.

The Nine-Day Revolution

For more than forty years, since the end of World War II, the once proudly independent nation of Romania was a Soviet satellite held in the brutal control of communist dictators. A whole generation of Romanians were trained to act like sheep under the wolves who ruled them. Over the years, communists threw hundreds of thousands of their suspected opponents into prison, where many of them died. Untold numbers of people starved as the government profited from shipping much of Romania's food abroad, and families shivered in the darkness as the government rationed heating and electricity. Civil liberties were taken away, churches and synagogues were bulldozed, schools were used to indoctrinate kids with the communists' warped views.

Romania's dictator since the 1970s, Nicolae Ceausescu, and his wife, Elena, didn't even try to act like they were of the people. Living in a palace in Bucharest, they spent extravagantly and behaved condescendingly while the population went on suffering. Hating the Ceausescus was a national pastime (as long as you muttered in secret), but apparently there was little the people could do. By every indication, Soviet–Eastern Bloc communism was here to stay.

Yet by the late 1980s, as Ronald Reagan had foreseen, the Soviet Union cracked under the pressure of keeping up the competition of the Cold War. To everyone's amazement, the Russians began to use words like *glasnost* (transparency) and *perestroika* (reform).

Following the cue, communist satellite regimes toppled in one Eastern European nation after another. Although information was strictly controlled within Romania, the people could follow outside events via Radio Free Europe. Romanians came to believe that maybe their situation was not hopeless after all. On the other hand, Ceausescu was a merciless dictator, and any Romanian revolt could easily come to an abrupt halt, just like the Chinese protest in Tiananmen Square.

One who caught the vision of a possible victory over the Soviet-backed Romanian communist dictatorship was a church pastor, Laszlo Tokes, in the western city of Timisoara. He pondered the times and his own role in them. Should he speak up? It could cost him and his wife their lives. It could cost the lives of many in his five-thousand-member congregation and close the church's doors. He chose the course of bravery. In his sermons, he began to denounce the unjust tactics of the nation's leadership.

The government responded with intimidation. Members of the internal security force made Sunday attenders of Tokes's church run their gauntlet when entering the church building. Once a service began, agents would stand in front of the sanctuary holding machine guns or dangling handcuffs. Hardly subtle threats.

Yet still the people came to listen to Tokes's bold sermons, nodding along.

In mid-December 1989, authorities came to the home of Tokes and his wife to load up the couple's belongings, intending to move them to a rural location where they wouldn't have so much influence. But the authorities never got inside the Tokes's door. Hundreds of church members had known what was coming and surrounded the home, denying entry to the government workers. Police turned water cannons on the resisters, but they endured it and refused to leave. In fact, others joined them.

Later that night, Tokes looked out his window to see hundreds of people massed in the street, each holding a candle in the darkness. Many lights of hope had been lit. The revolution had begun.

Two days later, goons broke into Tokes's church building, beat him bloody, and hauled him away for interrogation. But by now the resistance was strong enough to go on without its early leader. Massive crowds filled the central square of Timisoara. Pastors led the people in recitals of the Lord's Prayer. Citizens spoke aloud a word they had previously only dared think: "Freedom!"

Knowing what a threat all this was to his power, Ceausescu ordered armed troops and tanks to surround the square in Timisoara. On December 21, soldiers opened fire on the peaceful protestors. Shrieks rang out, and groups dashed this way and that for safety. Dozens of innocent civilians died of gunshot wounds.

Still, the crowds regathered. In fact, despite numerous outbreaks of government-initiated violence, the revival spread to other locations in the country, even the capital, Bucharest.

The next day Nicolae and Elena Ceausescu fled in a helicopter, and a member of a quickly organized group called the National Salvation Front became acting president. Back in Timisoara, a pastor named Peter Dugulescu announced the news and led a crowd of over one hundred thousand in a prayer of gratitude. As soon as the state surrendered control of the media, one revolutionary cried out on national television, "God has turned his face on Romania! We've won!"[3]

On Christmas Day, the Ceausescus were executed, and it was really all over.

In the decades since the revolution, Romania has had its problems, of course, but it's still a vibrantly democratic country, known as "the Tiger of Eastern Europe" because of its strong economy. More than three-quarters of the population identify as Christians. The stunning church-led revival has produced permanent gains for all Romanians. A journalist summed up: "What began as a congregation's protest in support of its beleaguered pastor became the nine-day revolution that cost thousands of lives but brought *libertate*—freedom—to the Romanian people."[4]

Why shouldn't churches start revolutions? When you think about it, the Christian church *is* a revolution.

Whitecaps On a Tsunami

A different perspective can alter everything. Take the stock market.

Someone can show you a graph of a downturn in the stock market over the past few weeks or months, and you can think, *Oh no, I should have sold my investments! We're all going to be ruined!* But zoom out to the last hundred years, and what will a graph of stock market values look like then? The only impression you will come away with from this perspective is one of steady growth—up and to the right. Market corrections in our lifetime that frightened millions are represented as barely noticeable dips. Even the Great Depression is revealed as an aberration in the overwhelming trend. This is why the great investors, like Warren Buffett, have always invested for the long term, not focusing too much on last quarter's report.

This is the way we ought to approach culture and history.

God has always told us to take the long view. If you look at the near term (as almost everyone does), the headlines can invoke fear. That shocking crime! This moral transgression! The other example of corruption! We have our own wars and rumors of wars, as every generation does. Reporting nervously to one another, we say it must be the end of the world. But what if the current status is just a data point on a much bigger chart?

Again, I'm not trying to minimize the bad things that are going on—evil is evil. I'm saying that we need to keep our heads and put it all in perspective.

Social Improvement

Things seem bad now, but what if you were living in 1941, when an unprepared America was about to plunge into the biggest war the world has ever seen?

We tend to think every election that rolls around in our day is the most important one in history. Really? More important than the election of 1860, which would determine whether civil war would start?

Or go back further than that in world history to see how much worse things have been.

The number of abortions today is appalling...but I'm thankful we don't see children being thrown into the flames as a sacrifice to the idol Molech.

We're disturbed by immorality...but in ancient Greece adult-child sex was all the rage, and in ancient Rome orgies took place in imperial palaces.

The pressure on Christians is rising today...but then Emperor Nero had Christians torn apart by wild animals, nailed to crosses, and burned to provide lighting at night.

It's shocking how many cases of human trafficking exist in our day...but for thousands of years slavery existed institutionally on every populated continent of the globe—it was just smart business.

In his bestselling book, *Factfulness*, Hans Rosling marshals evidence for ways in which the world is getting better, contrary to our presumptions. Did you know, for example, that average life expectancy rose from thirty-one years in 1800 to seventy-two years in 2017? Or that deaths from natural disasters are a tiny fraction of what they used to be a century ago? Or that the share of the world's population living in extreme poverty has dropped by at least half since 1993?[5]

Almost everywhere you look around the world, the improvements are so great that they've become invisible—we take them for granted. Even where societies are struggling against tyranny and corruption, at least the people have *standards* that were unknown in pagan cultures of the past.

Here's what we must recognize: most of the social progress in the last two thousand years can be accredited to the family of faith. The early Christian believers, during the Roman Empire, scoured the dumps to save babies that had been left to die, elevated the status of women, and brought an end to the gladiatorial games. Christians preserved the light of literacy during the Dark Ages. Then in the Middle Ages they began the founding of hospitals and universities. Modern science might never have developed without a basis in Judeo-Christianity's rationality and linear view of history. Christians were responsible in large measure for the development of capitalism, representative government, the separation of government powers, the Protestant work ethic, and modern charitable giving. Christians were leaders in the abolition of slavery in Britain and elsewhere, brought a halt to cannibalism in places like Fiji, and stopped *suttee*— the burning of widows on their husbands' funeral pyres—in India. Hundreds of the world's languages might not have been put into writing if it weren't for Christians bent on translating the Bible.

While reciting this history, I don't forget the tragic truth that professing Christians have been guilty of doing much harm over the centuries, nor that non-Christians have made crucial contributions to progress. My point is that, globally, the advances of the last two thousand years for the common good would never have come about as they did without Christianity.

This isn't a cause for pride in humanity but a call to give praise to God. None of it would have been possible without the Gospel.

Growth in Christianity

Christianity has grown from the 120 people who received the Holy Spirit at Pentecost to one-third of the world's population, if you include everyone who self-identifies as Christian. Globally, there are about 2.5 billion Christians, with growth occurring at an estimated 1.31 percent annually (faster than the total population's growth rate of 1.20 percent).[6] This kind of growth must at least have been a part of what Jesus foretold when he compared the kingdom of God to a tiny mustard seed that eventually becomes a huge and beneficial plant. The kingdom of God may spread invisibly, like yeast in dough, but it spreads in such a way as to affect the whole (Matthew 13:31–33).

Although the percentage of Americans who call themselves Christians is shrinking, the size of the American church is still huge. "In terms of raw numbers," points out the Center for the Study of Global Christianity, "Christians are still the vast majority (nearly 250 million in 2010, compared to 44.6 million nonreligious)."[7] About 60 million Americans meet pollsters' definition of evangelical.[8]

And that's just the picture in America. In many other places, Christianity is growing—fast.

In 1970, about 43 percent of all Christians lived in Africa, Asia, or Latin America, or what is called the *global South*. The other 57 percent lived in the *global North*, including America. Today, the balance has flipflopped, with 68 percent of Christians in the South and 32 percent in the North. The number of Christians in the global South alone could exceed 2 billion people by the end of this decade.[9]

The worldwide church is still grappling with the implications of this shift in the center of gravity for Christianity. But one thing is for certain: if we want to get a proper perspective, we've got to look not just throughout history but also around the globe. Even if there has been a stumbling in Christian identity in the West, it has undeniably been taking hold south of the equator. The wind of the Spirit blows where He wills.

So Much More than the Turning of a Tide

Perspective. Don't look at just *now*. Look at the whole sweep of the Christian era.

Don't look at just *here*. Look at the whole world.

If we're seeing things myopically, it can seem like our culture is facing the perfect storm. But stand back and take the large view, and you'll see our current problems are like whitecaps on a tsunami of the advance of the Gospel washing across the whole planet.

The earth will be filled with the knowledge of the glory of the Lord,
as the waters cover the sea. (Habakkuk 2:14)

You Win

A question we sometimes ask ourselves is, why doesn't God just solve all our problems—completely, all by Himself, right now? After all, He's *almighty*. He doesn't *need* anyone's help, and no one could stand in His way.

Sometimes He reminds humanity of His power to act independently and overwhelmingly, such as when He sent a flood to the destroy the population of the wicked, or parted the Red Sea, or collapsed the walls of Jericho. But for the most part, He chooses to involve His people whenever ground needs to be taken for His cause. For whatever reason, God wants to involve us in His story, to give us roles in His drama.

Like any good story, the drama of the kingdom of God in history contains heroes and villains. The heroes must deploy their bravery, and the villains sometimes get the upper hand. There are moments when hope seems lost and there's no chance of coming back...and then the impossible happens. It's thrilling! It's meant to be that way.

If I can speculate for a moment, it seems to me that God not only wants us to be brave so we can meet the challenges He lays out before us; He also gives us challenges because He wants us to develop bravery. Becoming more courageous, and acquiring other virtues, is part of our character development (and I mean that in both senses). We become larger, grander, more human humans as we dare and strive and fail…and win. Heroes and heroines, potentially, every one of us.

That's why it's so sad when Christians are operating with a vision of defeat. The remainder of their script for this world says, *Things get worse, then it's over.* I've learned a little something about storytelling in my career, and I can tell you that, as drama, this stinks. Imagine how disappointing *The Lion King* would be if Simba decided to stay in his *hakuna matata* lifestyle in the oasis and did nothing to prevent Scar from ruling evilly over the Pride Lands.

If you have a vision of victory, the drama is much, much grander. This story doesn't end in disappointment; it ends with roaring applause and cheering from Heaven.

What if this national setback is really a divine setup for a spiritual comeback led by the family of faith? By now, I hope you're ready to answer without reservation: *It is!* If you can make the shift from pessimism to optimism, from discouragement to confidence, that's going to be a watershed in your life. It's almost true to say that gaining a vision of victory *is* the win.

And now, just when I've hopefully got you thinking big, get ready to turn the telescope of your perspective around, facing it not toward the ongoing and ultimate victory of Christ but toward the deepest recesses of your own heart. Because that's where your own personal drama starts.

CHAPTER 6

The Inside-Out Strategy

A man cannot govern a nation if he cannot govern a city.
He cannot govern a city if he cannot govern a family. He cannot
govern a family if he cannot even govern himself. And he cannot
govern himself unless his passions are subject to reason.

—HUGO GROTIUS

Once we have a vision of victory before us, we're ready to translate that vision into reality. Now is the time to choose our targets and attack! Decide where your passions lie and where you have the opportunity to change policy or culture, and take your first steps. No more delay or preparation. Get moving and act now.

Wait, wait! I'm only fooling you.

I'm going to be getting to the "act now" stuff in the next chapter, but the practicalities of living out our God-given bravery start in another place entirely—not *out there*, but *in here*. Before we can heavenize earth, our hearts must be heavenized.

It's always been a temptation to focus more on *what people do* than on *who they are*. That's the outside-in perspective. Jesus was clear about the primacy of the heart. "The good man brings good things out of the good stored up in his heart, and the evil man brings evil things out of the evil stored up in his heart. For out of the overflow of his heart his mouth speaks" (Luke 6:45). That's inside out.

The twice-born brave dare to look in the mirror. They stare into the eyes of the serpent of sin with the seven heads of pride, greed, wrath, envy, lust, gluttony, and sloth, and they crush it through personal repentance. God will put them in charge of greater things later, but first they have to be faithful in small things.

If we want to challenge a culture gone astray, we need to first look at the condition of our own hearts. Trust me, as counterintuitive as it may seem, and despite the risk of possibly stalling our momentum, we *cannot* skip this stage if we want our courage to produce the right kind of change in the right way.

To start, if we look at our hearts, do we even see a love for God in there at all?

Are You a CHRINO?

If there is any group that certain Republicans are more down on than liberal Democrats, it's got to be those they call RINOs—Republicans In Name Only, taken to mean "traitors to the conservative cause." Likewise, Democrats have their DINOs. I'm much less concerned about these apparent imposters than I am about CHRINOs—Christians In Name Only.

Some people think they are Christians if they call themselves Christian and align with a certain politician, platform, or party—or even watch a certain news channel. After all, they get angry at all the right stuff. They've got to be Christians!

Not so fast.

Jesus knew what was in the hearts of men and women. He also knew the future. Looking ahead to Judgment Day, He said something sobering…and frankly troubling. "Many will say to me on that day, 'Lord, Lord, did we not prophesy in your name, and in your name drive out demons and perform many miracles?' Then I will tell them plainly, 'I never knew you. Away from me, you evildoers!'" (Matthew 7:22–23).

Jesus was talking about people who do amazing spiritual acts. And they do it *in Jesus's name!* But there's a problem: they don't "know" Jesus, and He doesn't "know" them. When it comes time to discover their ultimate destination, Jesus casts them away from His presence. What a shock that must be to them!

I don't think Jesus was talking about people who deliberately fake being followers of Jesus; I think He was talking about people who genuinely believe they *are* followers of Jesus. Even leaders in the church. But Jesus called them "evildoers," so if anyone were to dig around in their motives and behaviors long enough, it would become apparent they were really living for themselves, not for Christ.

So, are you a CHRINO?

I'm not suggesting we need to live in constant self-doubt and worry about our eternal destination, but on the other hand, if we're going to call ourselves Christians, it's wise to make sure that we really are. "Examine yourselves to see whether you are in the faith," said the apostle Paul; "test yourselves" (2 Corinthians 13:5). You'll need to do this work by looking at your own soul and seeking God's perspective through prayer. These questions may help.

- What are you really trusting in to make things better? A certain politician? The next election? A winning strategy? A legislative package? The state of the economy? Or Christ?
- Do you love your enemies or hate them?
- Is defeating the other side a goal in itself for you, or do you want what is best for all?

+ Gospel or political ideology—which guides you more?
+ Which is your higher allegiance: to the kingdom of God or to the United States of America?
+ Do you *know and treasure Christ Himself* through faith, or do you really just *identify with Christianity* as a religion?
+ While your *words* mark you for a Christian, do your *actions* do the same? Even those actions not visible to the public?
+ Are you living by faith or by sight? Are you living for the praises of God or the praises of people? Are you living to serve or to be served?

If you don't know Christ, it won't do any good to protest, "Lord, Lord, did we not expose the flaws of wokeness in your name? Did we not in your name speak up at school board meetings and carry signs at pro-life marches?" He will say, "I don't know you. Away from me!"

Our hope abides in the fact that He welcomes all who come to Jesus in true faith, trusting and submissive as little children.

And that is only the start of our career in repentance, if we want hearts that serve as founts of goodness for the world.

My Own Personal Revival

The early days of 2021 were a strange time for everybody, with COVID resurging in the land. This wasn't long after my pastor friend performed his mock striptease. By this time, restrictions and protocols meant to deal with the virus had evolved, but they were still intrusive and increasingly objectionable. In many cases, businesses were still boarded up, schools still closed, church services still banned. The isolation was getting to everybody. Would this pandemic never end?

Meanwhile, the bizarre events and consequences of January 6 in Washington unfolded on television, soon to be followed by the inauguration of Joe Biden. The Left eagerly anticipated the first one hundred days of the new administration, and the rest of us were left with our unease. I began thinking, *What are we doing sitting at home under a virtual house arrest, just waiting for this next hundred days to unfold? As the family of faith, what's our hundred-day plan?*

Spending time in my Bible, I eventually made my way to 2 Chronicles 7:14, where God is speaking: "If my people, who are called by my name, will humble themselves and pray and seek my face and turn from their wicked ways, then I will hear from heaven, and I will forgive their sin and will heal their land." I said to myself, *That's it. Our problem is not politicians. Our problem is not a virus. Our problem, as the people of God, is our own wickedness and failure to keep our eyes on God.*

So I came up with a plan for myself. For the next hundred days, I would light a campfire in my backyard, broadcast a live video, and humble myself publicly, praying aloud with the nation and talking about the forgotten secret that made America so blessed and prosperous and free. I unpacked the contents of a book called *The American Covenant: The Untold Story* by my friend Dr. Marshall Foster. I called it the American Campfire Revival. Anybody could watch via Facebook Live, and eventually tens of thousands were doing just that every evening.[1] From what I heard from viewers, a lot of people who watched American Campfire Revival discovered with me the same need to look inward to reforming themselves first before they'd be able to look out and reform the nation.

It's so easy to criticize the "bad guys" for what they're doing to our society, when we'd do better to stop and think that maybe we've got some responsibility. The nation as a whole seems to be moving on from Christianity, but are *we* faithful to God? We despise the drift of morality in our society, but how are *our* morals? The state of the family might be bad and distorted, but are *we* giving our best efforts toward our spouse and kids?

In the context of the popular verse 2 Chronicles 7:14, we find a harsh warning from God about what can happen to His people if they are unfaithful. Solomon was dedicating the newly built temple, and so it was a happy time, yet in the midst of this God said there might come a day when He would allow Israel to be defeated by foreigners and the temple to be reduced to rubble. Why? Well, it wouldn't be the foreign enemies who would primarily be to blame. Instead, it would be because His own people forsook Him. Once they realized their own guilt, they would have the opportunity to humble themselves, pray and seek God's face, and turn from their wicked ways...and *then* God would forgive them and heal their land.

America is not the unique chosen nation of God, like Israel was, so we don't have the same kind of relationship with God as they did. But we have the American Covenant—our history of commitments, promises, and prayers to God, our form of government based on Christian principles, and our legacy of faithful men and women who bravely sacrificed so much for the cause of liberty. For our failures to live up to this covenant, we have a responsibility to repent and then to recommit to following His ways in our nation.

At the same time, we should be honest about our failings to our fellow citizens.

The family of faith today gets a lot of criticism for being hypocritical and hard-hearted. I think much of that is unfair and comes about, really, because people don't like the uncompromising messages of the Word of God that we convey. But to the extent that we really do deserve an unfavorable reputation, having failed to show the kind of love and consistency that Jesus did, then getting the planks out of our own eyes before removing the specks from others' eyes will at least lift the justification for others' negative reaction to us.

Having a heart that's right with God and with people will instill two qualities in us that second-birth bravery can't get on without: humility and love.

The inside-out strategy has upside-down values.

An Appeal to Heaven

When I see multicolored pride flags flying, especially over public buildings, I often think about the time when George Washington commanded that a humility flag should fly.

Known as the Pine Tree flag, it features a plain white background, a green pine tree in the center, and the words "An Appeal to Heaven." It may have flown for the first time at the Battle of Bunker Hill. We know for certain that in 1775 George Washington gave the order for this flag to be mounted on American naval vessels in Massachusetts Bay. From then on, it was one of several flags used during the Revolutionary period.

The species of pine tree portrayed on this flag is the *white pine*, common in New England, and this was not a random choice. Years before the Revolution, surveyors for the Royal Navy began marking the best white pine trees in the colonies for use as masts in British ships. This meant colonial foresters were prevented from selling their trees freely. And so, like the tea spilled into Boston Harbor, the white pine became a symbol of resistance to the king's oppression of his American subjects.

The phrase "An Appeal to Heaven," used as the flag's motto, was popular among the early patriots and came from a work by the philosopher John Locke in which he refutes the divine right of kings. Locke argues that, if you are in a situation where you don't have a fair justice system to which you can appeal when wronged, then you can take your appeal to a higher court—you can "appeal to heaven."[2]

In other words, Locke asserts the right of revolution, with God to determine the outcome.

I like to think of appealing to Heaven in a somewhat different way—as putting us in a place of humility. For atheistic humanists, people are at the highest level of authority, and they believe we should be relying on our own wisdom and judgment in all things. That's pride. The family of faith doesn't look to ourselves for what is right and just but instead to Heaven, to God.

Pride is the root and source of all other sins. Lucifer was cast out of Heaven for his pride. In his serpent guise he tempted Adam and Eve by inviting them to "be like God" (Genesis 3:5). Pride went before the Fall. And today, whenever anyone tries to effectively take the place of God by being their own ultimate ruler and authority, they are following in the same satanic line.

In certain situations there can be such a thing as justifiable satisfaction in oneself or one's community, but pride in the sense of taking credit we don't deserve, or of putting ourselves first, is always condemned in Scripture. "Whoever exalts himself will be humbled," said Jesus, "and whoever humbles himself will be exalted" (Matthew 23:12). Jesus's values are right-side up; they only look upside down because the world was knocked off its moral axis through the rebellion of Genesis 3.

Being brave is not about us and building our empires. It's all about serving others. If that's not the case, then what makes us any different from tyrants who are trying to impose their values on the rest of the people?

General George Washington did something at the end of the Revolutionary War that may have been as significant as anything he did in his military role—he went home. To Americans, he was the hero of heroes at the time, and there happened to be a power vacuum in the nation; the general could easily have seized civil control. In fact, King George of England was astonished to learn that he would not have a counterpart by the same name in his former colonies. A few years later, the expected scenario played out in France when another general, Napoleon Bonaparte, co-opted the French Revolution for himself by placing an imperial crown on his own head. George Washington, however, was more concerned about service to his young nation than about pursuing selfish ambition, and he was just happy to get back to the home life and agricultural work awaiting him at Mount Vernon.

In the tradition of the American Covenant, the man who gave the order for the Appeal to Heaven flag to wave wanted America to seek its greatest good in the King of Heaven, not in an earthly king. Surprisingly (from the worldly way of thinking), it was in this way that he went on to become the first president of his country and to do much good for nations and generations yet to come, rather than going down in history as an example of a power-obsessed ruler, like Napoleon.

If we desire to have influence in our communities and our nation, are we putting others before ourselves? Are we seeking, not attention for ourselves but advancement for the cause of God? Are we recognizing that our progress comes from God's gifts to us and not from our own achievements? Are we trying to help others without looking down upon them or forgetting our own flaws? The pathway to strength is humility. Strength without humility is tyranny. Similarly, bravery without humility is arrogance.

And there's a second quality that, if possible, is even more out of step with our present-day culture and even more crucial to a bravery that does good.

Healing Hatred

Several years ago, I was in Washington, DC, at a "restore America" rally. At one point, an older African American couple came up to the microphone and shared the heartbreaking story of how their young son had been murdered in a gang shooting. Following this loss, the only thing that kept them going was their unwavering faith in a God who promises to bring good out of evil.

Next, the couple introduced a young man, who also told his story. He had joined a gang when he was young, accidentally killed someone in a drive-by shooting, and was put in juvenile detention for manslaughter. He said that, while he was in detention, he was visited by the couple who had just introduced him. They revealed to him that they were the parents of the boy he had killed. They had come to tell him that they didn't hate him and that they had been praying for him and wanted him to know about a God of forgiveness and new beginnings.

When the convicted killer got out of prison, that couple legally adopted him as their son and raised him in their home. Why did they do this? It would have been one thing if they had just forgiven the young man—that would be extraordinary but conceivable—but what motivated them to make him their own son? That's the kind of difference that being a Christian is from the ways of the world.

With tears in his eyes, the young convicted killer talked about the power of loving your enemies and the new life that he received by being introduced to the God of love and mercy.

Jesus had the highest ethical standard. Loving people who are on our side is one thing; loving people who are against us is another. Here are Jesus's words on the matter:

> Love your enemies, do good to those who hate you, bless those
> who curse you, pray for those who mistreat you. If someone

strikes you on one cheek, turn to him the other also. If someone takes your cloak, do not stop him from taking your tunic. Give to everyone who asks you, and if anyone takes what belongs to you, do not demand it back. Do to others as you would have them do to you. (Luke 6:27–31)

Remember that Jesus didn't just *say* to love your enemies. He actually *did it*. And who were His enemies? Well, they included the soldiers about whom He prayed, "Father, forgive them, for they do not know what they are doing" (Luke 23:34). But more relevantly, *we* were His enemies. "God demonstrates his own love for us in this: While we were still sinners, Christ died for us" (Romans 5:8). The wrath of God stood against us as people in rebellion against the King of Heaven, but Christ went to the cross for us anyway, extending His salvation to us out of love.

Loving one's enemies sounds like a great idea...as long as we're talking theory, or as long as it's someone else who has to do the loving. When we have an actual enemy—someone who is actually out to harm us—that's another matter. Jesus had actual enemies. And we will too, if we're serious about revolutionizing a hostile culture.

Being brave is going to get tough. We're going to get angry and want to retort. We're going to get hurt and want to hit back. It's *real* easy to start hating, even if we started out with the best intentions of being loving. So the one piece of advice I give people of faith who are having a hard time because they're taking a public stand for truth and liberty is this: hold on to your compassion.

Hold On to Your Compassion

I've been involved in my share of controversies over the years, but believe it or not, I'm not a controversialist by nature. I don't go looking for conflict. I don't like it.

I'm a peacemaker. I'm a bridge builder. Whoever you are, I want us to be friends. I want to meet up with the drag queen, the atheist, the social justice warrior, and I want to find some common ground while we talk frankly and respectfully about our differences. But it doesn't always go down like that.

In 2012, I went on Piers Morgan's interview show, and he asked me what I thought about same-sex marriage. I told him I didn't support it and held the biblical perspective that same-sex relations are not in alignment with God's created order. Morgan came at me hard for this position—the first time I'd been treated like this on camera. Afterward, I was feeling shaken but believed that basically I'd handled it well. I thought I'd been clear in articulating a position that is based on a four-thousand-year-old moral standard given to us from Moses and held by civilizations all over the world and that, until recent years, had been standard even among Democrats in this country. And I thought I'd done it without being unkind or disrespectful to anybody.

I could not believe it when I started seeing the reactions to the interview. GLAAD tried to paint me as out of step and as belonging to a minority that was clutching an outdated viewpoint. Some of my fellow *Growing Pains* cast members rushed to distance themselves from me.[3]

This was the first time I got hit publicly like that. I'll be honest, it hurt.

In the years since, I've had plenty of opportunities to develop a tougher skin. I've learned that, when we are trying to be faithful, we've got to hold on tight to our compassion. Watching my reputation smeared, and wondering how it would affect my relationships and work prospects, it would have been easy for me to backtrack from the biblical position on homosexuality in order to regain acceptance from my industry. Even more seriously, it would have been easy for me to get mad and stop caring about people who disagreed with me—and that would really have been a sign of failure.

I'm no better than anybody else. Whatever I know about the truth, it has been revealed to me, just as to us all, in the Word of God. God loves all people, and so no matter how painful the personal attacks get, I still need to see my angry opponents as people with God-given dignity in need of a Savior. Speaking the truth isn't enough; I have to speak it in love (Ephesians 4:15). It helps to remember that my struggle isn't really against human opponents but against the spiritual forces of evil in the heavenly places. My detractors aren't the enemy; they're the opportunity.

This isn't an issue only for people in the public eye. It's an issue for the whole family of faith as we try to do our part in the reformation of the culture.

Working to change a society is going to get confrontational, whether we want it to or not. Our bravery is going to be met with scorn, ridicule, and worse. It's an angry, hateful world out there; let's not make it worse. If Jesus held on to His compassion all the way up to death on a cross, we can hold on to ours. The ungodly know not what they do.

Our goal is to perfect the art of loving others, even the people who are against us. Despite our occasional failures, a genuine effort at love may prove more persuasive than any of our arguments. But even if we don't change anyone's mind, we will keep loving others, because that's what God has done for us.

The Seer

While I was making my documentary about the Pilgrims, Marshall Foster introduced me to the National Monument to the Forefathers, in Plymouth, Massachusetts. Located a short distance from the burial ground of the Pilgrims, and surrounded by a residential neighborhood, it's not a shy statue. In fact, it's the largest solid-granite monument in the world. Reaching eighty-one feet into the sky, it's an imposing presence on its hilltop.

The first thing you notice about this monument is the huge figure on top: a robed woman representing faith. Her right hand is pointing upward, toward the heavens. She's signifying that we're to look above for hope, for guidance, for authority. The woman is holding a Bible, with the pages opening, to show that we consult the Word of God to find the truth, insight, and guidance we need. The star on her forehead represents the wisdom that results.

At the base of the monument are four facets, each richly figured and clearly labeled: Morality, Education, Law, and Liberty.

The last figure, representing liberty, is…well, he's a serious stud. In fact, when I think about those unashamedly masculine, yet self-controlled, men I describe in chapter 4, they look like Liberty Man in my mind. He's wearing soldier's garb and holding a sword, though he's seated comfortably and not currently engaged in battle. We know he's a victor, because he's holding broken chains in his left hand, showing that he's already been freed from subjection to tyranny. He's wearing the skin of the lion of oppression that he's killed. He's ready to fight again, if necessary, to defend liberty in a new generation, but right now he's enjoying the fruits of the freedom he's won…and judging by the smile on his face, it feels pretty good.

In a way, Liberty Man is the end stage. He's the goal. He's who all of us who were born to be brave, both men and women, are turning into. But before we get to be like him, we've got to be more like the woman on the statue who represents Morality.

Madame Morality is a dignified, strong-looking person in a flowing gown, rather like the woman on the better-known Statue of Liberty. The figure here, though, is seated and holding both the Ten Commandments and the New Testament, identifying the source of our ethical framework—God's unchanging Word. That's not surprising, since we've already seen the same symbolism with Faith. But as you pay more attention to Morality, you realize there's something strange about her. She has no eyes! Where her eyes should be are blank disks. What's going on here? All the other figures on the monument have eyes; did the sculptor simply forget to give Morality eyes? No. Marshall explained the real reason to me.

Morality doesn't have eyes, because she's looking internally, to the transformation of her heart first, which then produces good works on the outside. Her morality is far from being an anything-goes, change-with-the-times philosophy like we're faced with today, but neither is it an enforced obedience to a code that makes us do what we're told whether we want to or not. We obey God freely, from the heart. Humility, love, and all good things flow from a transformed spiritual self. It's that inside-out strategy again.

The best forms of law, education, and liberty—and everything else good we might pursue in our second-birth courage—come within reach if first we tend to the heart. Marshall said:

> Two thousand years ago, the Almighty unleashed upon the world the most powerful world-changing force ever known to man— the self-governing Christian. This new individual freed from the shackles of sin and guilt was armed with the only weapon that can subdue the earth and its institutions—the Word of God. He became the bulwark of a movement that was begun by God Himself and about which Jesus said, "The gates of hell shall not prevail against it" [Matthew 16:18].
>
> Historically, whenever this new creation (a true believer) has understood God's instructions and has applied them to all spheres of life, he has gained dominion over his circumstances. He has progressively proven that "whoever is born of

God overcomes the world" [1 John 5:4]. He is not dominated by history; he shapes it according to God's will.[4]

If you live in New England or are going to visit there, stop in Plymouth and take a look at the National Monument to the Forefathers for yourself. With apologies to the monument's neighbors, I hope my readers in large numbers will beat a path of pilgrimage to this underappreciated national site. If you carry your copy of *Born to Be Brave* with you as a signal, you might meet a new friend. You might even wish to salute him or her, because you're both in the same army.

CHAPTER 7

Army of Compassion

Let us stand fast in what is right and prepare ourselves for trial.
Let us neither be dogs that do not bark, nor silent onlookers,
nor paid servants who run away before the wolf. Instead,
where the battle rages, let us find ourselves. Run towards the roar
of the lion! Run towards the roar of battle! That is where Christ's
most glorious victories shall be won!

—BONIFACE

If Ezekiel 37 is ever turned into a movie, the CGI team will love working on it.

That's the chapter of the Bible where Ezekiel has a vision in which he prophesies to the bones of a long-deceased army lying uncovered on a former battlefield. The bodies come together from the inside out: first the bones reassemble themselves with an eerie rattling sound; then tendons, flesh, and skin appear and begin to stretch to cover the skeletons; and finally breath enters the corpses and "they come to life and stand up on their feet—a vast army" (see verse 10). Can you picture the scene in your mind? Creepy. And dramatic for sure.

Written after Israel had been conquered by Babylon and seemed to have no future, this prophetic vision gave assurance to the exiled and the captive that God's people would one day live together in blessing under the Messiah. This prophecy wasn't originally referring to America, obviously. But I believe it provides symbolic imagery for *every* instance, in *every* nation and generation, where a people of faith think that they and their way of life are extinct, or almost extinct, and then God brings them back to life and influence.

At the very beginning of our nation, the small band of Pilgrims may have looked puny and pitiful when they landed on Plymouth Rock, but in fact they were combatants in the cosmic struggle for the hearts of men. Historian Marshall Foster said, "The voyage of [the Pilgrims] that summer of 1620 would initiate a peaceful revolution, following the selfless strategy of their Savior, which would free more people, both spiritually and physically, than any army in history."[1] They showed our nation, and other nations watching from around the world, how to maintain a society blessed with Gospel and governmental liberty.

Today God is assembling a new army in America. We may not think there are enough of us left to fill the battalions, but that perception is not reality. As we look around carefully, we see that God, in His grace, has created more of us than we thought, living in different places, passionate about different issues, blessed with different gifts, but all yearning to see a cultural transformation in our land. Through this vast army, God will be able to do immeasurably more than all we ask or imagine, according to His power that is at work within us.

We are not a literal army, marching with physical weapons in our hands. We're not trying to destroy those who think differently from us, but rather, we're trying to show them the compassion of Jesus and the possibilities of forming a better society around godly precepts. As I like to put it, *we are a loving army of compassion*.

This army is on the march, with others rallying to our banners as we go. We're not just going along with political conservatives' attempts to reverse the actions of progressives—we're the family of faith, and God is expecting us to *lead* the comeback. It's essentially a *spiritual* comeback, targeting tyrannical humanism at its core and revitalizing the Judeo-Christian worldview for our nation.

I can't tell you how it's all going to go, and I don't know what your part in it is going to look like (I'm still trying to figure out more fully what my *own* role should be), but I do know that it's not just a *pragmatic project*; rather, it is a *supernatural campaign*. After we have had our hearts transformed (see chapter 6), we're ready to turn outward. And as we do so, we have three divine gifts to guide and help us in bringing love to a culture deformed by attempts to order society with human gods at the center.

Commandments.

Community.

Calling.

The Straight Stick

The Pilgrims arrived on this side of the ocean possessing copies of the Geneva Bible, published from the 1570s. This was the first mechanically produced, mass-marketed Bible translation in English for individual use. I find it fascinating that, once the Bible was given to the common men and women, it changed everything, because they started thinking for themselves. They said, "This is what the Word of God says. We must follow it, not what the king or anyone else says, if they contradict the Word." It was because of the Bible that the Puritans created a reform party within the Church of England, and it was the Bible they used to shape their new community in New England.

As America moved closer to independence, the Bible continued to exert a powerful influence. In fact, the Bible was by far the most accessible and authoritative text for eighteenth-century Americans. Probate records show that, if someone left just one book in his or her estate at death, it was very likely to be the Bible. Political scientist Donald Lutz investigated the sources cited by America's Founding Fathers and discovered that *one-third* of their quotations came from the Bible, more than any other source or school of thought.[2] Even those who might have been illiterate or too poor to own a Bible were exposed to more Scripture than most modern-day people, with the average colonist in New England listening to about seven thousand sermons in a lifetime.[3]

Over time, though, that Bible centrism has faded. If you want a bellwether for this trend, look no further than how our universities have decoupled from Christianity over the years. Of the first 108 colleges in America, 106 were formed by Christians, often for the preparing of ministers. This included the earliest college, Harvard, whose original motto read, "Truth for Christ and the Church." (Over the years, the motto has shrunk to "Truth.") Today our universities are some of the most anti-Christian, and least free, places in our nation. To many academics, the Bible is (to borrow their jargon) a tool for patriarchy and systemic racism and misogyny that could use a trigger warning on practically every page.

In America as a whole, we have lost sight of the Bible, and therefore it is no longer affecting our morality, our education, our government, or even our churches and seminaries, as it used to. This creates the gap that allows the assumptions of secular humanism to flood in and take the place of biblical thinking. How did we get to a place where good has become evil, and evil has become good, until we're living with wrong-side-up morality? It's because of the loss of the Word of God.

So, how do you convince a crooked culture that they're crooked when they have come to believe that the standard for what's right is whatever they think? Nineteenth-century preacher Charles

Spurgeon gives the strategy beautifully: "If a crooked stick is before you, you need not explain how crooked it is: lay a straight one down by the side of it, and the work is well done. Preach the truth, and error will stand abashed in its presence."[4]

Even in a day when fewer are familiar with or respectful of the Bible, scriptural truth has an innate rightness and power that people often sense despite their bias. God has made us so that we resonate with His Word. Although all of us, before we are redeemed, suppress the truth by our wickedness, we all have the law written on our hearts and a conscience that bears witness to the truth (Romans 1:14–15; 2:14–15).

When Jesus was asked, "Is it lawful for a man to divorce his wife for any and every reason?" (a hot topic of debate in His day), He laid down the straight stick of Scripture. "'Haven't you read,' he replied, 'that at the beginning the Creator "made them male and female," and said, "For this reason a man will leave his father and mother and be united to his wife, and the two will become one flesh"? So they are no longer two, but one flesh. Therefore what God has joined together, let man not separate'" (Matthew 19:3–6, referencing Genesis 1:27 and 2:24). In this way He clarified truths about gender, marriage, and sexuality using the Bible.

We must be firm in our minds that the Word of God isn't going anywhere and it can never lose its power. The grass withers, and the flower fades, but the Word stands forever. God's thoughts are higher than human thoughts, and they never fail to accomplish the blessing God intends. All Scripture is God-breathed and is useful for teaching, rebuking, correcting, and training in righteousness. It is living and active.

Because of this solid biblical foundation, we can have the boldness to move forward in faith and obedience. The Word of God will not fail.

Using Scripture in public debates in our day takes bravery. We may be ridiculed, dismissed as outdated, or labeled haters merely by association with the Bible. But let's not fail to quote God's Word, retell its timeless stories, and do our best to base our thinking on its principles. Even if people don't accept scriptural authority, as we do, we're educating them about what the Bible says and bringing it back into the public discourse as a touchpoint for decision-making.

I believe that, over time, as we in the family of faith speak with compassion, grace, and courage, our words will lay down the straight stick of truth over the crookedness of humanism and progressivism, and the power of the Word will more and more have its effect in shaping our culture. But let's remember an important distinction: We don't use Scripture because it "works." If we fall into that kind of utilitarian trap, our motivation is really no different from that of anybody else who thinks they have the right message for the day. Furthermore, if Scripture ever appears *not* to work, we'll be tempted to modify it. So, changing someone's mind with the Bible isn't our number-one goal; *honoring God by speaking the truth is our number-one goal.*

And as we speak Scripture, who knows? It may be a milestone in the spiritual journey of someone who is on his or her way to following Jesus, because faith comes by hearing, and hearing by the Word of God.

The apostle Paul urged us to become "children of God without fault in a crooked and depraved generation, in which you shine like stars in the universe as you hold out the word of life" (Philippians 2:15–16). Our generation is messed up. Can we agree on that? This means our witness will stand out all the more, and influence more lives, if we're faithful to God and to the straight stick of His Word.

Home and Gate

To Jesus, all the commands of Scripture boil down to loving God and loving your neighbor. This gives us the perspective we should keep in mind as we are bringing the Bible to bear on the issues of our day. It is also why we can say with confidence that basing society more soundly on the Word of God is *good for all*, because it comes from love.

This doesn't mean applying Scripture is always easy or we'll always agree on how best to do it. We first must really know it, be saturated in it ("letting it dwell in us richly," as Paul says in Colossians), so that it forms our way of thinking and naturally springs from our lips. The average American spends *two hours per day* on social media and another *two hours per day* watching television; I think most of us could find more time to spend with the Word if we tried, reading devotionally, studying with reference tools, sitting under wise preaching and teaching. Also, we need to learn rules of application. For example, the modern republic of America is not the same thing as the chosen nation of Israel, and we don't play the same role in God's plans for history, so biblical commands to Israel don't simplistically transfer to America. The Bible does, however, show us the moral order of the universe (an order that atheistic humanists deny even exists) and helps us see how we can live in alignment with that order.

The commands are a gracious gift to us because they transform us and then enable us to transform the world as an army of compassion.

Twice a day, for thousands of years, faithful Jews have prayed the *Shema Yisrael*: "Hear, O Israel: The Lord our God, the Lord is one" (Deuteronomy 6:4–5). The Shema captures the essence of the Bible's unique form of monotheism. I find it meaningful that the Shema is embedded within a chapter of Scripture that talks about the themes that are at the heart of this book, namely *fearing God and not other people* (bravery) and *national blessing based on obedience to God's truth*.

As I look at how the Bible as a whole talks about itself, I see a process of the Word of God taking effect on people who are willing to submit to it. First, instead of being conformed to the (crooked) pattern of this world, we are transformed (straightened) by the renewing of our minds. We have the mind of Christ. Then the Word goes to our heart, which, biblically speaking, is not just the seat of our emotions but our spiritual self—literally, everything we are (Proverbs 4:23)! We hide the Word of God in our hearts so that we will not sin against God but rather live for Him. Next, we share the Word with our family, taking every opportunity to reinforce God's commands. We impress the Word on our children, talking about it when we sit at home and when we walk along the road, when we lie down and when we get up. The Word of God also guides us in a choice of vocation and permeates our lives on the job, and therefore the favor of the Lord rests upon us and He establishes the work of our hands.

If our lives are shaped by the Word of God and consecrated to the God of the Word, then biblical truths will permeate our public actions as well as our private ones. In the Old Testament era, Israelite elders would gather at a city gate to discuss community business, hear arguments for legal cases, and make public announcements. *Our* "city gates" are many, including the room where our town council or county board meets, halls of legislature, and courtrooms across the nation. In each of these places, and beyond, we can bring our Word-formed wisdom into action as we participate as citizens and perhaps as hired administrators or elected representatives.

Let me summarize how the living and active Word of God will circulate within you as you open yourself to it.

The Word of God enters your Head.
From there, it moves to your Heart.
Over time, it characterizes your Home.
And determines the work of your Hands.
As you go out and impact the wider world,
the Word will be your guide in the city Gates,
which represent the common life and Government.

We're able to bravely lead in the cultural changes to come not because we're so smart but because we have the commandments of God to guide us and to share with others. And equally, along with *the Word of God*, we have *the people of God*.

Where Are You?

At the time when I was doing book readings for kids at public libraries nationwide, a conservative Christian governor asked me to visit him at his office. He expressed support for what I was doing and said that, as long as he was governor, these kinds of events would be welcome in his state.

I thanked him for his backing. Then our conversation began to tread on some more sensitive areas. I knew that, in recent weeks, the governor had taken heat from some people in his own party for what they saw as his not standing up consistently enough for conservative causes.

"Did you see that line of people waiting to see me, when you came in?" the governor asked.

I told him I had. There were dozens of people in outer offices and down the hallway hoping to get a moment of the governor's time to pitch their causes.

"There's a line like that every day," the governor said. "And do you know what? There are more of them outside the building with signs, standing for their liberal causes. They make the noise. They're representing every progressive cause imaginable.

"Where are the conservatives?"

This was another reminder to me that conservatives have in many ways abandoned the field to progressives, giving up influence they might have *simply by showing up*. But what was more eye-opening to me was how *alone* this Republican governor of a red state appeared to be feeling. He wasn't getting the help, the encouragement, or the mere presence from conservatives that helps to keep our representative warriors strong.

If we're looking for reasons why men and women who get elected based on conservative campaign promises sometimes wobble on their convictions when they get into office, this might be one major reason. But *all of us* need support and encouragement to maintain our convictions and put them into practice.

When John the Baptist had been surrounded and supported by his disciples and followers, he'd had no trouble crying out, "Look, the Lamb of God, who takes away the sin of the world!" (John 1:29). But when John was alone in a prison cell, facing execution, he began to have second thoughts about whether Jesus really was the long-promised Messiah. Understandably, he didn't want to die for a mistake. Jesus quickly sent back a message of reassurance (Luke 7:18–23).

When someone is willing to be brave and stand up for change in our culture, we shouldn't just wish them well from afar. Like Aaron holding up Moses's arm that gripped the staff during the battle with the Amalekites, we should be lending our strength to bolster others' efforts in bravery.

As Christians we already enjoy the divine gift of community: we have our churches, our small groups, our ministry teams, and so on. These are not just therapeutic "support groups" but supernatural bodies. And yet, as we become more active, not just within our church zone but out there in the world, we will need more. As God moves you toward a mission, find a group of people who are passionate about the same things you are, and join them to pray together, encourage and advise (and if necessary rebuke) each other, and work together. I've got a band of brothers I talk with regularly in person or by phone to pray with and encourage one another in our work and family lives, and I couldn't do what I'm doing without them. The divine gift of community gives us a power that nothing else can replace.

It may be the oldest metaphor in human language, but after one hundred days of campfires, I can tell you it's still true that you have to keep the embers together to get a fire blazing.

Village Power

Although today Clapham is a fashionable district lying within the borders of London, in the late 1700s and early 1800s it was a rather ordinary, stand-alone village, with a modest brick building for its church. But when the local pastor, John Venn, began preaching strong biblical sermons with a social edge to them, more and more people got intrigued and came to hear. Many of these people were influential figures, including businessmen, bankers, writers, and members of Parliament. Eventually a community of like-minded Christians who wanted to change their world coalesced in this small community. Mocked by being called "the saints" in their day, they are remembered today as the Clapham Sect.

If you've seen the movie *Amazing Grace*, you know that one of the most memorable figures connected with this group was William Wilberforce, leader of Britain's abolition movement in Parliament. And one of Wilberforce's friends and mentors was John Newton, slave trader turned clergyman and writer of hymns that included the immortal "Amazing Grace." In the movie, an aging Newton says,

"Although my memory's fading, I remember two things very clearly: I'm a great sinner and Christ is a great Savior."[5] That, in a sentence, is the attitude of those who do brave things for God in their world.

Other leaders in the Clapham group included Granville Sharp and Thomas Clarkson, who, along with Wilberforce, were responsible for founding an experimental colony in Sierra Leone in 1787. Here the British resettled some of the African Americans they freed during the American Revolutionary War. The purposes of creating the Province of Freedom, Clarkson said, were "the abolition of the slave trade, the civilization of Africa, and the introduction of the gospel there."[6]

The signature achievements of the Clapham group were the passage of the Slave Trade Act of 1807, banning the trade throughout the British Empire, and the total emancipation of British slaves with the passing of the Slavery Abolition Act in 1833. But these Gospel-motivated activists were also involved in many other causes, including the transformation of Britain's primitive criminal punishment system and the placing of restraints on the exploitation of laborers. They founded several missionary and tract societies that spread the knowledge of the Word of God and the love of Christ throughout Britain and around the world.

Many of the harmful and degrading aspects of British society at the turn of the nineteenth century disappeared because of the prayers and preaching, organizing and legislating done by the Clapham group. Their deeply ethical, religious, and family-loving views characterized British society for years to come by helping to set Victorian morality. As one historian said, "The ethos of Clapham became the spirit of the age."[7] One small community in one small town, one group of brave and persevering Christians, learning together, worshiping together, working together, defined an entire age.

Jesus started with twelve men, and that group reproduced over and over again, like cell life, until today, when a third of the world's population calls itself Christian.

Today, here, what can one family, one group of friends, one local church, one nonprofit accomplish for God, in His power, if they do it *together*?

This sort of *community* is one of God's great gifts for the loving army of compassion. We've also looked at the *commandments* of God. And the last divine gift—the one that gives it all specific direction for each of us individually—is *calling*.

Hot Girl Saves Nation

The queen of Persia was a young woman who had been selected for her marriage, apparently, on the basis of her beauty alone, even though she possessed intelligence and social subtlety as well. Her name was Esther. As a member of the Jewish community who had stayed in the East after the enforced Babylonian exile had come to an end, she had kept quiet about her racial identity because of the prejudice against her people (anti-Semitism is an old, old story).

Then one day she learned that her husband, Emperor Xerxes (reigned 486–65 BC), had authorized genocide against the Jews within his empire. So she was faced with a decision. Would she try to intervene with the emperor on behalf of her people, or would she seek to preserve her own life?

This choice wasn't as obvious as it might seem. The emperor had a rule that anyone who tried to approach him without first being summoned would be killed. *This applied even to his wife.* Esther couldn't just lay a hand on her husband's shoulder and say, "Honey, I want to talk to you about this murdering-the-Jews thing." In that culture, the emperor and empress didn't have that kind of relationship. If she went to him without an invitation and tried to speak up for her people, there was a strong likelihood that the attempt would not only fail but also cost her life.

Esther was like many of us. She lived in a culture increasingly hostile to her people and their beliefs, but she herself was in a comfortable spot, and so her instinct was to not get involved if she didn't have to. It was easier to keep her faith identity on the down-low and just get along. For us, if we've got a job and a home and a family, and the culture is frustrating but bearable to us, we think, why not just stay out of it?

Esther's relative Mordecai gave her the cold truth: she wasn't really as safe as she thought. She would not be immune to the genocidal violence that was about to be unleashed. "Do not think that because you are in the king's house you alone of all the Jews will escape.... You and your father's family will perish" (Esther 4:13–14). And the same is true for us. If we hide ourselves and don't act, our culture will slide further, and no matter how comfortable we might feel today, or how safe a niche we believe we have carved out for ourselves, it's going to get more and more painful for us and our children and grandchildren.

Then Mordecai gave the other side. He suggested there could be a divine setup embedded in the cultural setback, and it might involve Esther in particular. "Who knows but that you have come to royal position for such a time as this?" Maybe her selection as queen was a pre-ordained calling to play a part in godly change. And for us… what if God has placed us where we are, with our special concerns, our special opportunities, because that is precisely where He wants us to do our part?

Who knows but that you have developed such a reputation in your medical career so that you can speak out against a one-sided perspective on vaccination?

Who knows but that you got that promotion at work so you would be in a position to argue credibly against the new corporate woke guidelines that are unfair, unsafe, and kill profit?

Who knows but that you were assigned to teach the ninth-grade health class so that you can present the benefits of abstinence until marriage?

Despite the risks, Esther agreed to approach her husband on behalf of the Jewish minority. "I will go to the king," she said, "even though it is against the law. And if I perish, I perish" (verse 16). This sounds rather fatalistic, and maybe that's how she was feeling at the time. But as we read in the rest of the book of Esther, she so cleverly undertook her mission that, in the end, not only did the Jews survive but they managed to eliminate their worst enemies. Esther was fine, and the Jewish people (and the empire as a whole) were better off because of her bravery fueled by faith.

While we do have a clear calling to bravely lead our families to live by the grace of God for His glory in our everyday lives, we may not always have a clear calling from God regarding specifically what He wants us to do in engaging the larger culture. But we can actively look for indications from Him. Maybe it is not something He speaks to us but something that becomes plain through our circumstances. The opportunity could be right in front of us.

Miracle Wall

Imagine that you are a Jewish person living in Jerusalem in the twentieth year of the reign of Artaxerxes, the emperor who followed Esther's husband, Xerxes, on the Persian throne. (For us modern folks, we're talking about 445 BC.) Your people are in the middle of a cultural setback so bad and so long lasting that it seems hopeless.

According to the stories told by the elders, your nation used to be proud and wealthy, strong and independent. But more than a hundred years ago, the Babylonians conquered Jerusalem, tore down the temple and the protective wall around the city, and took hostages back to Babylon with them. Since then, some of the exiles returned, and a new temple was constructed, but the city wall is still down. Every time you look beyond the outer buildings of Jerusalem you see a ring of rubble from the old wall, many of the stones still blackened where flames licked them during the long-ago destruction.

The downed wall is a constant reminder that your people are not free, being subject to the mighty Persians, and that's only the start of the problems. For as long as you can remember, the Jewish leaders collaborating with the imperial power have been corrupt and arrogant, lording it over the people. The religious leaders haven't all been as righteous as they should have either. Taxes have been excessive, stifling prosperity and growth. The people live in constant anxiety for their survival, because without that wall, any foreign power could march in at any time. It's a discouraging life, and your nation, as it currently exists, hardly seems worthy of the glorious God your rabbi preaches about every Sabbath.

Then one summer day you hear about an important Jewish man named Nehemiah who has arrived from the imperial capital. An official announcement says that he's organizing the rebuilding of the wall, and he wants to get started right away. Everyone has to help, grouped by families and communities. Your family has been assigned to rebuild a section of the wall not far from your home.

After your initial surprise and nervousness at this news, you begin to think it might be a good thing, a way to put some of your nation's shame behind it. The project might even be fun, since you'll be working together with your whole extended family, and there will be friends and neighbors nearby.

One thing, though. You've been told to keep a weapon with you at all times, and that's rather troubling, because you're a peaceable person by nature. But it makes sense: The nearby nations aren't going to like the rebuilding of the wall. They prefer Jerusalem to be weak and vulnerable. As you're working on the wall, who knows what armed bunch might come rushing over the hills toward Jerusalem without warning? You hope not, but you might have to use that old sword you found and sharpened.

As the days of hard work on the wall go by, however, no enemies appear; the fears seem unfounded and the sword a mere encumbrance. But one day, when your family has your section of the wall about halfway up, news begins sweeping across the city. The neighboring nations to the north and east are putting together an army to attack Jerusalem before the wall is completed! Work comes to a halt. Everyone is chattering and fearful.

Nehemiah gathers a crowd to give a speech. To you, he looks tired—it must be true what they say about him working harder than anyone. Nehemiah confirms the news about the enemy coalition, but he raises his voice to put iron in the spines of all listening: "Don't be afraid of them. Remember the Lord, who is great and awesome, and fight for your families, your sons and your daughters, your wives and your homes." His message is to keep going on the wall *and* be ready to fight, if necessary.

"Don't be afraid," Nehemiah repeats to himself. Yes, *bravery* is exactly what you need right now.

You and your family get back to the wall, trying to work faster. But the higher the wall rises, the more exhausting the labor becomes. Standing a shift of guard duty at night, in addition to working on the wall from sunup to sundown, doesn't help. You feel more exhausted than you've ever felt before.

And then there are the discouraging messages that keep circulating in the city. "The work is too much for us—we're exhausted and we can't keep going!" "The enemies are going to get here before we finish the wall, and they're going to kill all of us!"

Something inside you rebels against these negative views. *Do they want us to just give up?* you think, disgusted. You resolve to stop paying attention to the doomsayers. Nothing is going to prevent you from building this section of wall!

And all of a sudden, *it's done.* The entire wall, including the complicated construction at each of the gates, has been completed—in just fifty-two days. With everybody working on a piece of the project right in front of them, an "impossible" victory was achieved against all the odds. And you never had to use that sword you've been carrying around. It seems the enemy didn't have the stomach to fight over this wall after all.

Now, every time you look at the wall and see watchmen keeping guard on its walkways, or see gatekeepers letting traffic in and out in an orderly fashion, you feel prouder than you have ever felt about your city. You're more hopeful about the future for your children and grandchildren who will live here. You praise God for what He achieved through your people, and you know that anyone on the outside who hears about this miracle wall will have to reconsider the greatness of the God of Israel too.

Back to the present…

I'm not Nehemiah, but if I could speak like him for a moment, I would say this: Let's not be discouraged by the massive project of repairing the ruined "wall" of our own culture. None of us has to do it all. It's all about specialization and cooperation. Let's try to sense which piece of the "wall" near us God wants us to repair, and get to work on it. Let's do it alongside our families and friends, helping each other maintain confidence and keep a light heart about the work. Let's keep our mouths shut and not repeat unnecessary gossip or pessimism. But let's keep going. Remember that we're doing this not just for our own benefit but for the good of our loved ones and all people in this generation and those to come. Most of all, we're doing it because it brings God glory.

Lila Rose learned about the tragedy of abortion while being homeschooled and went on to join and then lead Live Action, a pro-life advocacy organization. She's been a pioneer in using undercover videos to reveal the truth about Planned Parenthood. She's building her section of the wall.

Peter Hitchens, brother of outspoken atheist Christopher Hitchens, was himself an atheist and socialist for years. Through a return to the faith he'd been taught in his childhood, he became a member of the Church of England as well as a conservative author and journalist. His is a powerful contrarian voice in a largely progressive United Kingdom. He's building his section of the wall.

Jackie Hill Perry was a lesbian "stud," in relationships with other women, when God drew her to repentance. In her book *Gay Girl, Good God*, she assures readers that God can transform lives and empower believers to resist temptation. Now a wife and mother, she expresses her faith through music, spoken word poetry, and writing. She's building the wall.

Joe Kennedy was a high school coach in Washington state who would pray on the field and welcome students who voluntarily chose to join him in taking a knee. Refusing to quit his prayers when his school system tried to shut him down, he lost his job. Through all the years of legal wrangling leading up to his victory before the US Supreme Court in 2022, he faithfully kept on affirming freedom of religion. A man building his section of the wall.

What part of the wall do you see in front of you?

Bravery Training

I was a teenage atheist. I had my life turned upside down when my then girlfriend's father and some other Christians were brave enough to listen to my rants about religion and talk through my questions and objections. Something strange started happening in my heart (familiar to me now as the Holy Spirit), and one day in 1987, I pulled my car over to the curb on Van Nuys Boulevard and begged God, if He were real, to save me.

My TV show *Growing Pains* was in the middle of its run when word started circulating among the cast and crew that Kirk had become "born again." I was visibly changing. I cleaned up my language and stopped joining in the dirty jokes and other crude behavior I used to enjoy on and off the set. Awkwardly but genuinely, I was trying to figure out what it meant to be both a follower of Jesus and the teenage star of a TV show.

The tension surrounding me rose to the surface when I began to have qualms about a few things I was seeing in the scripts of upcoming episodes. For example, in one opening scene Mike Seaver was supposed to wake up in bed next to a beautiful girl. He was to roll over and say, "What's your name again?" Later it would be revealed that he was only acting out one of his mother's vivid nightmares, but dream sequence or not, I didn't like the idea of viewers seeing Mike so casually in bed with a woman.

A few times I fought down my nervousness and went to the producers and writers to talk about having some scenes changed. They listened, and almost always accommodated my requests, but I was accused by some of being a religious brat, flexing celebrity muscle with older and more experienced people in order to occupy the moral high ground. I'm sorry to say some relationships that were important to me soured in ways they never recovered from.

At the time, I didn't understand the reaction I was getting. I wanted to say, "Why aren't you happy for me because I found God? Why are you getting mad at me when I'm just trying to keep our family show clean for the kids who watch it?"

I didn't know then that, when we're brave enough to stand up for godly things, it's *normal* to become a target (John 15:18–21).

And then, I need to take some of the blame myself. I was just a teenager and a new believer when I got into these conflicts. I didn't know much about how to choose my battles and fight them wisely. I didn't know how to let my speech "be always full of grace, seasoned with salt," so that I'd know how to answer each writer and producer (Colossians 4:6).

Years later, on the set of the *Growing Pains* reunion movie, I approached the producers and said, "Hey, I wanna let you know…a lot of years have gone by. I've thought a lot about what happened during those years and I know that I could have handled those situations more graciously than I did when I was seventeen. We had a lot of great years together, and I hope you can forgive me for any frustration I caused you."[8]

It was true: I could have handled it better, and I wish I had. But in a way, that's the whole point. I was *learning*.

Just like David's experience in defending his sheep against lions and bears helped him face Goliath later on (1 Samuel 17:34–36), we all have to go through bravery training. We don't necessarily even know we're enrolled in this education program. We might hate it, just like I hated to see the camaraderie on the *Growing Pains* set dissolve into mistrust. But we can be confident that in every less-than-perfect situation our perfect God is up to something, teaching us how to spot situations where we're called to be brave, how to do it boldly and effectively, and how to keep on trusting Him and treating others lovingly no matter what happens.

In your own efforts toward bravery, you'll learn over time, and make mistakes, and that's okay. The person who is engaging the culture imperfectly is being more faithful to Jesus than the person who sits at home saying it's hopeless. Inexperience and uncertainty are no reasons not to jump into brave acts of culture transformation with all your energy and eagerness. We can learn as we go, but we have to go in order to learn.

Remember, as a family of faith, we're *leading* the transformation of our society. We can do that, despite our human weaknesses, because of the gifts God gives us: His *commandments*, or the Word of God, to instruct us; the *community* of Jesus followers who form our family, our team; and the *calling* that God gives us to take on tasks He has already prepared us for.

This is how we make earth more like Heaven. And as we are faithful, we could see God rouse people here and around the world in ways we never dreamed we'd see.

CHAPTER 8

The Comeback

Oh! men and brethren, what would this heart feel if I could but believe that there were some among you who would go home and pray for a revival, men whose faith is large enough, and their love fiery enough to lead them from this moment to exercise unceasing intercessions that God would appear among us and do wondrous things here, as in the times of former generations.

—CHARLES SPURGEON

In the biopic *Harriet*, a minister named Samuel Green is helping a young Harriet Tubman plan her escape from slavery. "Fear is your enemy," says Green at one point in their conversation. "Trust in God."[1]

It would be hard to put more succinctly the message you and I need to hear today if we are going to be free from the spiritual and social chains that bind the twice-born citizens of our nation. *Fear is your enemy. Trust in God.*

You were born to be brave.

The amazing real-life history of Harriet Tubman (1822–1913) includes her personally rescuing seventy slaves during thirteen expeditions and leading an armed mission during the Civil War that freed more than seven hundred enslaved people. The deepest motivation for her brave works was her faith. As a child, she listened to Bible stories told by her mother and attended Methodist services conducted by the son of her white owner in eastern Maryland. She also attended revival meetings led by preachers such as the African American Jarena Lee. Later she became a practicing member of the African Methodist Episcopal Church.

Like Joan of Arc, Tubman had frequent visions that guided her choices. Once, for instance, when she was leading two enslaved men toward freedom, she suddenly felt that God was telling her to get off the road they were taking. She led the two men through an icy stream and got them to safety. She nearly died of pneumonia as a result, but it was worth it, because as it turned out, the escapees' master had put up an advertisement offering a reward for these men, placing it in a railway station close to where Harriet felt the Lord's command to leave the road.[2]

What's often overlooked about Harriet Tubman is that she came to faith in the late stages of a time known as the Second Great Awakening. This period of ongoing revival in the early nineteenth century led to millions of black and white Americans coming to follow Jesus. For the slaves, their taste of spiritual freedom in Christ deepened their hunger for physical freedom, and biblical stories, such as the Exodus, gave substance to their vision for an end to slavery.

The ending of slavery was just one of the major social consequences of the Second Great Awakening. If it hadn't been for this time of spiritual renewal, Harriet Tubman's life—and many other things in America—would not have been the same. And I believe the American experience in that period may have a lot to teach us about our own.

Life in America today isn't as dreadful as many of us conserva-tives have been imagining, and it doesn't merit the end-of-the-world prognostications we keep repeating to one another. But that's not to say things aren't bad and, in some ways, trending worse. This is why the family of faith is standing at a crossroads of decision: Will we squander our energies in complaining, turn our focus inward, wave the white flag of surrender, and wait for the Lord to Rapture us away? Or will we take a deep breath…and begin again, in confi-dence and faith, to build a freer, more godly and just society for the glory of God?

So much depends on our choice.

The present cultural setback could be a divine setup for a spiri-tual comeback led by the family of faith. And then, instead of ruin, we will see renewal in our lifetime. For this, we, like Harriet Tubman, need to recover our vision of victory and our birthright of courage and get to work at our calling.

The things I've been encouraging Jesus's army of compassion to do—reform ourselves first, rebuild our family life, then influence culture and policy in every way we can—are really an everyday duty or expectation of the people of faith. The more faithful and consistent we are in it all, the better we can transmit the Christian message and values from generation to generation. But in this chapter I want to suggest that there could be an even bigger potential outcome. Aren't we really yearning for not a moral maintenance program, not even incremental improvement in society, but *bold leaps ahead*? There's a name for that.

From Wokeness to Awakening

By the 2010s, progressives were using the term *woke* to differen-tiate themselves from those who hadn't "woke" up yet to the beauties and wonders of leftist ideologies on things like race and identity.

If you still believed in such outdated ideas as free speech and religious freedom, or equality of opportunity (as opposed to equality of outcome), or news without a filter of left-wing "fact checking," or the unchanging nature of the sexes, or accurate interpretation of the Constitution, or the positive benefits of capitalism, or the idea that there might be something wrong with rewriting history, you were slumbering in the past, like Rip Van Winkle.

Like many conservatives, I sometimes poke fun by applying this ungrammatical adjective to the foolish programs that progressives believe in with such grim fervor. And I find it interesting that there's a similarity between the term *woke* and the word that has long been used to characterize the periods of *real* progress in American history.

Awakening.

Terms like *revival, renewal,* and *awakening* are often used interchangeably, but to me *awakening* best expresses what I'm trying to portray as the highest outcome we can hope and pray for. An awakening is a time when the people of a land turn to God in large numbers through repentance, and as these people are transformed, they go on to transform their families and their culture in many different and dramatic ways. Spiritual revival in the church powers a cultural awakening to the ways of God.

Historians have detected five major awakenings in American history alone—times of spiritual revival that set off ripples of influence that didn't stop until they spread across the whole lake of national culture.

The First Great Awakening: Started about 1734

Revival in Britain spread to the American colonies with the work of ocean-crossing preachers such as George Whitefield. In New England, Jonathan Edwards developed a theology of revival still relied upon today. While greatly increasing the number of churchgoers, the Awakening also created a new unity among Jesus followers across denominational lines, which in turn led to the founding of many educational institutions and a booming in missionary efforts. Through the Awakening, Christians enjoying spiritual liberty would come to desire political, economic, and educational liberty, preparing the nation for the American Revolution that lay ahead.

The Second Great Awakening: Started about 1790

Following the establishment of America as a nation, revivals broke out in many places, such as western New York State, Logan County in Kentucky, and Harriet Tubman's eastern Maryland. Church membership soared again, and several new religious groups were formed. Preachers taught that believers should not only repent of personal sin but also work for the moral perfection of society. The Second Great Awakening birthed temperance, abolition, and mental health reform movements, among other initiatives. As pioneers moved ever westward, denominations created a religious and educational infrastructure for the frontier areas, including such new organizations as the American Bible Society.

The Businessmen's Revival, or the Third Great Awakening: Started about 1857

This revival began when lay missionary Jeremiah Lanphier started a prayer meeting over the lunch hour in New York City. The first day, only six men showed up. But at its peak, a year later, ten thousand men were meeting to pray at what came to be known as the Businessmen's Revival. The spiritual electricity radiated outward from New York to New England, Ohio, and other parts of the nation, affecting cities and rural areas alike. Crime during this period decreased, despite an economic downturn and massive unemployment, in part because wealthier Christians provided financial assistance to the poor. The greatest long-term effect of the revival was that it prepared the nation to endure the painful exorcism of the demon of slavery during the Civil War, and created bonds that assisted reunification afterward.

The Azusa Street Revival: Started about 1906

William J. Seymour, an African American pastor, was preaching in Los Angeles in 1906 when a revival broke out that lasted about a decade. Controversially, this revival featured "signs and wonders." White, black, and Hispanic Christians mingled in revival meetings in a way that was unusual at the time, forwarding racial harmony. With the sending out of missionaries, the Pentecostal movement was begun, now accounting for half a billion Christians around the world and still the fastest-growing segment of global Christianity.

The Jesus Movement: Started about 1968

As portrayed in the movie *Jesus Revolution*, this movement began among young people in the turbulent hippie days of the late 1960s. Influenced by charismatic theology, and welcoming a countercultural style, the Jesus movement came to involve large numbers of "Jesus freaks" on college campuses and elsewhere. It birthed churches and parachurch organizations and created contemporary Christian music and modern Christian media. Some members of this movement focused on rescuing their contemporaries from drug addiction and religious cults.

I'll do the math for you. 56—67—49—62.... Those are the periods of time between the estimated beginnings of these awakenings. Or in other words, according to this historical reckoning of American revival history, about every fifty to seventy years an awakening has broken out. You can do the final calculation on the time elapsed since the last major revival.

Are we due for another awakening? It's possible. I wouldn't dream of trying to hold the sovereign God to a pattern like this without some direct revelation from Him authorizing it. But it's *possible*.

Certainly, if there's such a thing as feeling the vibe of a time, then I and many people believe we're seeing the stirrings of what could be a momentous spiritual upheaval. I sense a restlessness in the family of faith for more of the power of God, and I see a dissatisfaction among unbelievers with the unpalatable feast served up by secular humanism. There's a widespread sense that things are *not right*. There's a desperate searching going on.

It's often when things seem to be at their worst that the greatest awakening lies ahead...and this may be one of those times. Plagues and epidemics have been harbingers of awakenings in the past, so in that sense even COVID-19 may yet do us some good![3]

We can't *create* revival, because that's a work of God. But we can *pray for it* and *position ourselves for it*—if God chooses to send it—through our courage, commitment to reform, faith in God and the victory of His cause, and all the rest of what I've been urging. God spoke 2 Chronicles 7:14 to Israel, not to America, but I think we can trust He still has the same heart of mercy today as then: "If my people, who are called by my name, will humble themselves and pray and seek my face and turn from their wicked ways, then I will hear from heaven, and I will forgive their sin and will heal their land."

The Kingdom of God and the United States of America

As hard as it may be for us to imagine it, North Africa was once a mighty stronghold of Christianity. After Jerusalem fell to the Romans in AD 66, Alexandria in Egypt for a while became Christianity's most important intellectual center, producing scholars like Origen, Clement, and Tertullian. The Christians were a major presence in several North African cities, including Carthage (part of today's Tunisia), which hosted international Christian councils. And one of the greatest Christian theologians of history—the fourth century's Augustine—was a church leader in what is now Algeria.

What about North Africa *today*?

North Africa is currently a stronghold of Islam. Indigenous Christian communities survive as religious minorities in Syria and Egypt, but long ago Christianity all but disappeared in northwest Africa.

Six hundred years of Christian history couldn't guarantee protection against the waves of Islamic invasion and occupation washing across North Africa. Is it credible that Christianity could vanish from *North America*, like it did from *North Africa*? I suppose the more likely scenario is that Christianity here, rather than vanishing, could fade, as it has already done in Western Europe. But is it *possible* that Christianity could disappear in the land of the Pilgrims, Jonathan Edwards, D. L. Moody, Billy Graham, Elisabeth Elliot, megachurches, ichthus bumper stickers, and currency imprinted with "In God We Trust"? Actually it is.

There is no spiritual manifest destiny in America. Christianity is not guaranteed to survive, much less thrive, on these shores. Our American Covenant, while renewable, is not unconditional. If people of faith make the wrong turn at the present crossroads, God could send us into our own Babylonian captivity or diaspora. A totalizing force, like secular humanism or Islam, could conceivably replace Christianity here.

The spread of Christ's influence in the world is a tsunami, but that tidal wave is *the kingdom of God*, not the United States of America. Although the kingdom's destiny is to occupy the whole world, that doesn't mean there won't be times and places where the flood recedes, leaving dry ground…and this *could* include our country. In that case the kingdom of God would continue to grow and transform human societies elsewhere, probably most dominantly in the global South. Maybe back in North Africa again!

Obviously I don't want to see Christianity die here—this is where I, my family, and my friends live. You don't want it either. Furthermore, by now I trust we both have a vision of victory, and so we should neither think nor act like the destruction of American Christianity will happen. I don't spend a moment worrying about that. But I believe we should keep in mind the *theoretical possibility* that Christianity could be shut down in this country rather than expanded.

Why?

Because it reminds us that our hope is not ultimately in this country and what happens here. Our hope is in Christ Himself and His plan, which is bigger than us and our family, bigger than our country, longer lasting than our generation. Religious historians tell us that the revivals around the world tend to follow an uprising of prayer, so let us pray for an awakening here at home and around the world, wherever God wants to send it, expanding the kingdom of God and bringing Heaven nearer earth by the power of the Spirit.

Meanwhile, let's check our passports to make sure we have the right citizenship—and it is a *dual* citizenship. Our primary citizenship is in Heaven (Philippians 3:20), but it is also incumbent upon us to be grateful, law-abiding, and vigilant citizens of whatever nation we live in. Sometimes there may be some tension between our two loyalties (notice that by heavenizing earth we're trying to reduce that tension), but there's never any question which citizenship comes first: our heavenly citizenship. This has always been so for the followers of Jesus.

A Christian named Mathetes, writing about a century after Christ's death, at a time when the church was misunderstood and persecuted within the pagan Roman Empire, struggled to put into words the way that genuine Jesus followers are *in* and *for* their earthly nations while ultimately being *of* the heavenly kingdom.

> [The Christians] dwell in their own countries, but simply as sojourners. As citizens, they share in all things with others and yet endure all things as if foreigners. Every foreign land is to them as their native country, and every land of their birth as a land of strangers.... They are in the flesh, but they do not live after the flesh. They pass their days on earth, but they are citizens of heaven. They obey the prescribed laws, and at the same time surpass the laws by their lives. They love all men and are persecuted by all.... They are evil spoken of and yet are justified; they are reviled and bless; they are insulted and repay the insult with honor; they do good yet are punished as evildoers. When punished, they rejoice as if quickened into life; they are assailed by the Jews as foreigners and are persecuted by the Greeks; yet those who hate them are unable to assign any reason for their hatred.
>
> To sum it all up in one word—what the soul is to the body, that are Christians in the world.[4]

Did you detect some of the themes we've already considered? Righteousness not out of mere obedience to law but from the heart? Misunderstanding and persecution? Love for enemies? Seeking to do good for all (that soul-to-the-body-in-the-world thing)?

It's our citizenship in Heaven that puts our citizenship on earth in truest perspective. American Christianity *may* expand. The kingdom of God *absolutely will*.

Christian Multinationalism

I am an American and I have addressed my words in this book mostly to Americans. But these messages apply in their essentials to all Christians, in every region and nation of the world. If we are in Christ, then whichever of God's beautiful ethnic creations we are a part of, and within whatever national borders we may happen to dwell, we have been a part of God's plan from ages past and are called to live out our grace-born bravery where we are.

America has a glorious Christian heritage that it is popular now to dismiss or to try to run away from. We can debate whether it's wise in these days to label America a Christian nation or not, and what that would mean. But there's no being honest with history if one denies that Christianity has historically been the dominant influence within America's family, religious, educational, and government institutions.

I heard a pastor once state (rightly, I believe) that America's problems are *universal* but her successes are *unique*. We have struggled, and still struggle, with common, self-inflicted wounds from pride, greed, and selfishness as well as with outside forces that would steal our freedom. Nevertheless, this nation has produced religious and political liberty, educational opportunity, and economic well-being for its people, regardless of their gender, skin color, or immigration background, to a degree that has no equal in history.

These benefits don't just go back to the Declaration of Independence and the Constitution. They go back further to the Pilgrims, the Puritans, and other people of faith who founded the American colonies with intentions to bring heart-transforming blessings to all people and reflect God's glory in their civil societies. And they go back even further to the biblical Christianity recovered by the Protestant Reformers. Truly the Word of God came out to this land of America and has not returned void.

To this extent, it is fair to say America is exceptional, though of course far from perfect.

At the same time we recognize God's blessings brought to the world through America, let's not forget that other nations have strong Christian roots that can be nourished for future abundance and harvest. Did you know that the apostle Thomas spent his last years in India, and today there are Christian churches along India's west coast that still honor Thomas's memory and take him as their inspiration? Or that Christianity, carried along by Roman believers, may have gone as far north as Britain before the end of the first century AD? Or that St. Patrick converted all of Ireland in the fifth century? This stuff is all a lot older than the *Ninety-five Theses* or the Mayflower Compact!

Some nations around the world have benefited from a significant Christian influence in the past but have seen that influence diminish in recent decades. There is no reason why such trends cannot be reversed. I know many faithful followers of Jesus in Western Europe, for example, are praying and believing for just that.

Other nations have had far less of the advantage of Christianity over the centuries and are still in desperate need of the Gospel today. In some nations (notably Islamic and communist nations), Christianity is restricted if not outlawed. Only 19 percent of people around the world who belong to another religion even know a Christian.[5] As many as one hundred thousand Christians are martyred for their faith every year.[6] Yet despite such sad facts, *no* nation is beyond the reach of the Gospel.

In arguing that Christianity belonged in the Greek world as much as within the Jewish context, the apostle Paul said, "The God who made the world and everything in it is the Lord of heaven and earth.... From one man he made all the nations, that they should inhabit the whole earth; and he marked out their appointed times in history and the boundaries of their lands. God did this so that they would seek him and perhaps reach out for him and find him, though he is not far from any one of us" (Acts 17:24-26).

It was no accident that any of us was born where we were. Wherever we find ourselves, we are a part of God's bigger plans for human cultures and societies, and we have been commissioned to make God and His ways better known to our neighbors. God has already revealed that the eternal Gospel will make its home among every nation, tribe, language, and people (Revelation 14:6). That's a guarantee.

Can we not do our best to promote biblical influences for our own individual nations while at the same time remembering it is the kingdom of God, spreading throughout all nations and outlasting every one of them, that is our highest affiliation? I deny that we must do only one or the other.

All we men and women of the family of faith were born to be brave regardless of where we live. Let each of us have the courage to build on the Christian tradition we have available to us and recommit to transforming our nations to glorify God and spread His blessings. Regionally and globally, let's learn from each other, support each other, and grow stronger connections so that we can do the work of bravery together. And let's get busy right now, making the most of the opportunities before us.

Own the Agenda

The progressive elites today are like a 120-pound lion tamer armed with nothing more than a cracking whip—their intimidation. Filled with the Spirit of God, the family of faith is a pride of big, strong lions. Why are we letting the lion tamer control us and tell us to perform the way he wants us to? Let's give a massive roar and leave this progressive circus, go out to live our lives, wild and free.

Years ago, my wife and I decided that, instead of sending our kids to a public school system that had abandoned biblical truth as its foundation for seven hours a day, five days a week, while trying to inoculate them with biblical truth in our limited time with them at home, we would homeschool them. We would take their education completely into our own hands. We've since then met thousands of other parents who are sacrificially educating their kids at home, in Christian schools, or in creative hybrids that allow them to present the straight stick of Scripture instead of the crooked stick of what our current culture promotes.

When I was reading my children's books in public, I could have chosen some safe environments, such as churches or Christian events. But instead I chose to take my story hours into public libraries, in progressive areas of the country, where drag queens had already been invited before me. The impact was so much greater that way.

Instead of just pointing fingers at Scholastic for promoting books with unacceptable messages, I'm helping to create a complete alternative for school book fairs, SkyTree.

Hollywood won't fund a faith-based "Mr. Rogers" type of show for kids? Okay. So then we'll crowdfund *Adventures with Iggy and Mr. Kirk*, along the lines that helped make *The Chosen* an outsider entertainment phenomenon.

Like everybody else, I'm just making up the best strategies I can as I go. I'm trying to be imaginative in my solutions. And my experience has reinforced my impression that we need a mindset change that's bolder, requiring more faith. Not just *tinkering* to make a bad system work a little better but *transformation* to produce something new. Leading instead of following. Setting the agenda. Conquering with creativity.

One beautiful thing here is that the most dramatic changes are likely to come from the most overlooked people.

Nobodies from Nowhere with Nothing to Offer

A lot of people in the family of faith feel like nobodies from nowhere with nothing to offer. If that's you, I'm thrilled to have you in the army of compassion, because it's very likely God will use you more than He will the egotist impressed with his own qualifications or the "influencer" busy showing off her videogenic presence.

You don't have to be a prominent figure like the general George Washington or the parliamentarian William Wilberforce to accomplish something big, though God obviously used those men and many other prominent people in history. You certainly don't have to be a Hollywood actor, like me. The most common category of people that God uses to make a difference are "nobodies," as long as they have hearts surrendered to Him and have activated the bravery He's given them. That describes the ex-slave Harriet Tubman. That describes the Pilgrims. That describes the lowly monk Martin Luther. And lots and lots of others throughout history.

In choosing David over his more impressive older brothers to become king, God said, "The Lord does not look at the things man looks at. Man looks at the outward appearance, but the Lord looks at the heart" (1 Samuel 16:7). I guess God's got a fondness for underdog stories, just like most of us do. He uses the foolish to confound the wise, gives strength to the weak, invites the last to cut in line and step right up to first place.

Men and women who seem like the heroes of history to us were often just simple people doing something they hoped was worthwhile in their corner of the world, never dreaming it would be talked about hundreds of years later. Likewise, today's game changers are probably not going to show up on CNN News tomorrow. We may not see the impact of this mother, or that teacher, or the other candidate for local office until history reveals it far down the road.

Have you considered that *you* may be that person? People in future generations may talk about what you did when you thought nobody saw or that it wasn't making much of a difference. So it doesn't matter if you're not getting attention now. In fact, there are times when you should deliberately keep your "acts of righteousness" out of the limelight so that the reward comes from God, not from human recognition (Matthew 6:1–4). The quality of your courage and tenacity will be revealed over time. And that's better than fine, because the goal is long-term growth within God's plan, not self-promotion.

I don't know about you, but for me this is frankly a relief after living in a culture that's more and more about getting noticed, finding fans and followers, and instant sharing and commenting and counter-commenting on everything. There's a stealth quality about a career of true bravery that's...well, kind of fun. It's one indication to me that we must be on the right track.

The kingdom of God has an inside-out strategy and upside-down values. It also has bottom-up growth. Woke humanism is top-down, with the elites trying to force the rest of us to accept what they are sure is right, forging their alliances with corporate partners and celebrity friends and putting technocrats in place to run the day-to-day show. Christianity is bottom-up, as the Spirit of God works invisibly in people whom others would ignore or denigrate.

This was the conflict back at America's beginning. The skeptics said, "How are you going to run a country without a king?" Our patriots said, "The people will run it themselves." The scheme could work because we actually *did* have a King, a heavenly one.

We still do. Our American Covenant may have suffered some unraveling, but it can be woven together again. As we lay down our hearts to God in our thousands and our millions, this may be the time He sends a new awakening to the land. That's something we could never create with our individual, self-focused efforts. It takes God working through His whole army of compassion, nobodies and all.

Heroism Calls

Briell Decker was eighteen years old when she became Mormon cult leader Warren Jeffs's sixty-fifth wife (out of an eventual total of seventy-eight).[7] Often bound and drugged, she was a prisoner in the 28,000-square-foot, forty-four-room house she shared with about half of Jeffs's wives and dozens of children. Following several failed attempts, she eventually managed to escape the Colorado City, Arizona, home by jimmying open a locked window and running barefoot to safety.

After Jeffs had gone to jail for child sexual assault, Briell discovered that, as a legal wife, she had a claim on the property where she had once been held against her will. Receiving ownership of the property through the court system, she partnered with the church in which she had recently come to embrace the Gospel—the Phoenix Dream Center—and together they converted the former domestic prison into a place of refuge for other women leaving the polygamous Fundamentalist Latter-Day Saints (FLDS).

The Dream Center, based in both Phoenix and Los Angeles, is what Pastor Luke Barnett likes to call a "blue-collar church," meaning they're focused heavily on work to help the needy on the nearby streets and out in the world. They have some of the most effective ministries in the nation to stop human trafficking, end childhood hunger, and lead people through addiction recovery. The church's tagline—"Find a need and fill it, find a hurt and heal it"—could well serve as the motto of the Brave Nation's Army of Compassion.

Today, if you were to visit the remodeled former Jeffs home, now known as the Short Creek Dream Center, you would find numerous women who have chosen to leave the FLDS with their children.

The women are receiving counseling for their trauma, getting the education they had been denied, and laying the groundwork for a better future for their families by learning job skills and budgeting. The success rate for the women's independence, measured one and a half years after graduation from a transitional program, is an incredible 95 percent. One of the residential aides deeply involved in this success is none other than Briell Decker, and her now redeemed and happy life serves as an inspiration to the other women.

The current directors of the Short Creek Dream Center are Konstance and Luke Merideth. Luke happens to have a fondness for superhero stories and owns several adult-sized superhero costumes. One day, some volunteers from out of town who were staying at the Dream Center compound asked if they could wear the superhero costumes while helping out in the center's food bank, which supplies more than half of the community with food. Luke agreed, and patrons received free groceries from the likes of Captain America and Green Arrow that same day. It was all just lighthearted fun.

Or was that really all it was?

One of the food bank patrons that day was a girl with a sad face. Susie (not her real name) was nineteen years old and still in high school because of a cognitive delay. She had recently been married to a man in his seventies who had moved to Colorado City solely because he knew its reputation and wanted to have sex with a teenager. Susie's parents had colluded with the old man in making this marriage happen against the wishes of their daughter. As the girl sat in a car with her siblings going through the food bank line to accept groceries, she kept casting glances at the "superheroes" on hand to help. Their comic-book identities connected with notions of rescue in her mind. An idea was birthed.

That night, after dark, Susie knocked on a side door of the Short Creek Dream Center and asked to be allowed in.

Welcomed inside, she was initially reserved and wary but gradually warmed up. She explained her situation to some of the staff and volunteers. They sympathized and asked her what she wanted to do. She said, "I don't want to be that man's sex slave anymore. Can you help me leave him?"

At Susie's request, five people—including some of those same people who had been dressed up like superheroes earlier in the day—drove her over to her house. The police had been notified, but since no crime had been reported to them, officers waited across the street and said they wouldn't come in unless they heard gunshots or screaming.

Fortunately the outcome was not that violent.

Susie escorted two of the men into her kitchen and then went to gather some of her things in a plastic bag. Her husband came out of a back room, saw what was going on, and became irate. He yelled at her, "Where are you going?" But when the security manager from the Dream Center—a big man who had formerly been in the military—showed himself in the hallway, the husband settled down.

Susie was emboldened by her support. She told the old man, "I'm leaving and there's nothing you can do about it."

She finished gathering personal effects, and just minutes after it had begun, the rescue operation was over.

Susie stayed with some extended family members who were supportive of her decision to leave the marriage. She repeatedly thanked the Dream Center team for their help.

Her husband went to jail.

Briell Decker is a model of bravery. So is Susie. And those people who had been wearing superhero costumes just for fun, *and then went on to carry out a real-life rescue*, found that through Christ's power they had the makings of heroism themselves.

The Early Church

Remember the story with which I opened this book? The day I put on my bulletproof vest and stepped out to face opponents with curses in their mouths and vengeance in their hearts at that public library in Washington, DC, I was feeling anxious. But I didn't let my fear control me. I really cared about those people who hated me, the families who were coming to my reading event, and others who would hear about it all in the news and draw their own conclusions. This love for others is not something I can take credit for. Left to myself, I would be just as much a self-centered hedonist as anybody else. But God has loved me through His Son (I feel it every day), and therefore I love others. I will keep stepping out to do risky or costly things on behalf of the Gospel.

How about you? Will you join me?

I'm telling you, *glory lies ahead!*

As you now know, I don't vibe with those who say the world is destined for inevitable decline. The kingdom is winning, not losing. It's expanding, not shrinking. The Gospel of Jesus Christ redeems the whole world. Jesus defeated the power of sin, death, the devil, and Hell. The Gospel does not kneel and it does not faint. No power, no principality, no darkness can defeat the Spirit of God working through His people on Earth. Jesus Christ is King over all creation for all time. When we take the long view of history, and look around us globally, we see that truth, beauty, and goodness are winning. Darkness (what's left of it) is on the way out.

The rumblings of a new American awakening are already being felt in our hearts. I can smell the fragrance of the new creation in the air. Something is happening in the consciences of men and women all around us. Eyes are opening. Ears are hearing. People are beginning to stand.

This is what it feels like when a move of God happens. We were born to be brave, and *this* is the reason.

Endnotes

Chapter 1: The Setup

1 Valerie Richardson, "D.C. Public Library Trolls Kirk Cameron with Rainbow Flags, LGBTQ Books," *Washington Times*, March 31, 2023, https://www.washingtontimes.com/news/2023/mar/31/dc-public-library-trolls-kirk-cameron-with-rainbow/.

2 *The Lion King*, directed by Roger Allers and Rob Minkoff (Disney, 1994).

3 Samarveer Singh, "What Rank Did Lia Thomas Stand at While Competing in the Men's Swimming Division?" Essentially Sports, March 22, 2022, https://www.essentiallysports.com/us-sports-ncaa-news-what-rank-did-lia-thomas-stand-at-while-competing-in-the-mens-swimming-division/.

4 Riley Gaines, "The Moment Riley Gaines' Life Was Turned Upside Down," Fox News, https://www.youtube.com/watch?v=8AY08gbZSbE.

Chapter 2: Heavenizing Earth

1 For more on Alfred, see Marshall Foster, "Alfred the Great," parts 1 and 2, *World Historical Journal*, May/June and July/August 2018.

2 Quoted in Foster, "Alfred the Great," Part 2, July/August 2018.

3 Quoted in Benjamin Merkle, *The White Horse King* (Nashville: Thomas Nelson, 2009), 199. The Golden Rule is found in Matthew 7:12.

4 Merkle, 234.

5 "What is the principal intention of this commission; to *disciple* all nations. *Matheµteusate—'Admit them disciples'*; do your utmost to make the nations Christian nations;' not, 'Go to the nations, and denounce the judgments of God against them, as Jonah against Nineveh, and as the other Old-Testament prophets' (though they had reason enough to expect it for their wickedness), 'but go, and *disciple them*.' Christ the Mediator is setting up a kingdom in the world, bring the nations to be his subjects; setting up a school, bring the nations to be his scholars; raising an army for the carrying on of the war against the powers of darkness, enlist the nations of the earth under his banner. The work which the apostles had to do, was, to set up the Christian religion in all places, and it was honourable work; the achievements of the mighty heroes of the world were nothing to it. They conquered the nations for themselves, and made them miserable; the apostles conquered them for Christ, and made

them happy." Matthew Henry, *Matthew Henry Bible Commentary*, Matthew 28, https://www.christianity.com/bible/commentary/matthew-henry-complete/matthew/28.

6 Abraham Kuyper, "Sphere Sovereignty," in *Abraham Kuyper: A Centennial Reader*, ed. James D. Bratt (Grand Rapids, MI: Eerdmans, 1998), 461.

7 Thomas Jefferson, "Jefferson's Letter to the Danbury Baptists," January 1, 1802, Library of Congress, https://www.loc.gov/loc/lcib/9806/danpre.html.

8 Russell Kirk, "The Errors of Ideology," in *The Politics of Prudence* (Washington, DC: Regnery Gateway, 2023), 1.

9 T. S. Eliot, *Notes towards the Definition of Culture* (New York: Harcourt, Brace, 1948), 31.

10 Dave McNary, "California Gov. Gavin Newsom Shows Support for George Floyd Protestors," *Variety*, June 1, 2020, https://variety.com/2020/tv/news/gov-newsom-sympathy-george-floyd-protests-1234622479/.

11 Sam Kestenbaum, "Since This California Church Began Flouting Pandemic Restrictions, Attendance Has Surged," *Washington Post*, February 26, 2021, https://www.washington post.com/religion/2021/02/26/godspeak-calvary-covid-rob-mccoy/.

12 Rachel del Giudice, "How This Pastor Resisted Government to Keep His Church Open During COVID-19," *The Daily Signal*, July 23, 2021, https://www.dailysignal.com/2021/07/23/how-this-pastor-resisted-government-to-keep-his-church-open-during-covid-19/.

13 "Pastor Rob McCoy Strips to Keep Church Legal in CA," YouTube, https://www.youtube.com/watch?v=XSkVdaBnS k kI4.

Chapter 3: Reporters and Reformers

1 Example: Isaiah 30:1–5.

2 *Monumental: In Search of America's National Treasure*, directed by Duane Barnhart (CamFam Studios, 2014). See https://monumentalmovie.com.

3 William Bradford, *History of Plymouth Plantation* (New York: Effingham, Maynard, 1890), 17.

4 You can visit the reconstructed Plimoth Patuxet plantation and *Mayflower II*. See https://plimoth.org/.

5 "Lastly, whereas you are become a body politic, using amongst yourselves civil government, and are not furnished with any persons of special eminency above the rest, to be chosen by you into office of government; let your wisdom and godliness appear, not only in choosing such persons as do entirely love and will promote the common good, but also in yielding unto them all due honor and obedience in their lawful administrations, not beholding in them the ordinariness of their persons, but God's ordinance for your good; not being like the foolish multitude who more honor the gay coat than either the virtuous mind of the man, or glorious ordinance of the Lord. But you know better things, and that the image of the Lord's power and authority which the magistrate beareth, is honorable, in how means persons soever. And this duty you both may the more willingly and ought the more consciously to perform, because you are at least for the present to have only them for your ordinary governors, which yourselves shall make choice of for that work." "John Robinson's Farewell Letter to the Pilgrims," July 1620, Pilgrim Hall Museum, https://pilgrimhall.org/pdf/John_Robinson_Farewell_Letter_to_Pilgrims.pdf.

6 "In the name of God, Amen. We, whose names are underwritten, the Loyal Subjects of our dread Sovereign Lord King *James*, by the Grace of God, of *Great Britain, France*, and *Ireland, King, Defender of the Faith*, &c. Having undertaken for the Glory of God,

and Advancement of the Christian Faith, and the Honour of our King and Country, a Voyage to plant the first Colony in the northern Parts of *Virginia*; Do by these Presents, solemnly and mutually, in the Presence of God and one another, covenant and combine ourselves together into a civil Body Politick, for our better Ordering and Preservation, and Furtherance of the Ends aforesaid: And by Virtue hereof do enact, constitute, and frame, such just and equal Laws, Ordinances, Acts, Constitutions, and Officers, from time to time, as shall be thought most meet and convenient for the general Good of the Colony; unto which we promise all due Submission and Obedience." Mayflower Compact, November 11, 1620 (Old Style), https://www.mayflowercompact.org.

7   William Bradford, *Of Plymouth Plantation*, para. 333, https://www.gutenberg.org/files/24950/24950-h/24950-h.htm. Spelling modernized.

8   John Winthrop, sermon, "A Model of Christian Charity," January 1, 1630, https://genius.com/John-winthrop-a-model-of-christian-charity-city-on-a-hill-annotated.   Winthrop was alluding to Matthew 5:14–16. The true city on a hill is the kingdom of God itself, but every community of Christians should strive to be the same kind of landmark for Jesus wherever they are.

9   "The First Charter of Virginia," April 10, 1606, The Avalon Project, https://avalon.law.yale.edu/17th_century/va01.asp.

10 "A Declaration by the Representatives of the United Colonies of North-America, Now Met in Congress at Philadelphia, Setting Forth the Causes and Necessity of Their Taking Up Arms," The Avalon Project, July 6, 1775, https://avalon.law.yale.edu/18th_century/arms.asp.

11 John Adams, "From John Adams to Massachusetts Militia," Quincy, Massachusetts, October 11, 1798, https://founders.archives.gov/documents/Adams/99-02-02-3102.

12 Marshall Foster, "Chaos or Christianity," *World History Institute Journal*, spring 2023.

Chapter 4: Arise, Warrior!

1   Jordan Peterson, "You Should Be a Monster," Jordan Peterson Motivation, https://www.youtube.com/watch?v=-gYpCIbZjUQ.

2   Quoted in Mike Cali, "Jonathan Isaac Explains Why He Stood During National Anthem," Orlando Pinstriped Post, SB Nation, July 31, 2020, https://www.orlandopinstripedpost.com/2020/7/31/21350233/orlando-magic-jonathan-isaac-national-anthem. For the full story, read Jonathan Isaac, *Why I Stand* (Nashville: DW Books, 2022).

3   "About," UNITUS, https://weareunitus.com/pages/about.

4   Jonathan Isaac, interview, "Influencing Culture: Stories of Impact," *Takeaways with Kirk Cameron*, TBN, October 23, 2023.

5   Joshua 2:24; 3:7, 10; 4:10; 6:27; 10:14, 42; 13:6; 14:12; 21:44; 23:3, 10.

6   Dale Ralph Davis, *Joshua: No Falling Words* (Fearn, Ross-shire, Scotland: Christian Focus, 2010), 18.

7   "Where It Started," Red Truck Men, https://redtruckmen.org/#history.

Chapter 5: A Vision of Victory

1   Ronald Reagan to Richard Allen, "My theory of the Cold War is: We win and they lose." Cited in H. W. Brands, *Reagan: The Life* (New York: Anchor, 2015), 254.

2 "How U.S. Religious Composition Has Changed in Recent Decades," Pew Research Center, September 13, 2022, https://www.pewresearch.org/religion/2022/09/13/how-u-s-religious-composition-has-changed-in-recent-decades/. As the percentage of Christians has dropped, the percentage of Americans who claim no religious affiliation (the "Nones") has risen steeply to 29 percent. This is clear evidence that Christianity is in a battle for worldview dominance with secular humanism.

3 Donald G. McNeil Jr., "Romania's Revolution of 1989: An Enduring Enigma," *New York Times*, December 31, 1999.

4 Tom Keppeler, "Romania: The Persecuted Church: Heart of the Revolution," *Christianity Today*, February 5, 1990, https://www.christianitytoday.com/ct/1990/february-5/romania-persecuted-church-heart-of-revolution.html.

5 Hans Rosling, *Factfulness: Ten Reasons We're Wrong About the World—and Why Things Are Better than You Think* (New York: Flatiron, 2018), 55, 110, 277.

6 Center for the Study of Global Christianity, Frequently Asked Questions, "Which Is Growing Faster, Christianity or Islam?" https://www.gordonconwell.edu/center-for-global-christianity/research/quick-facts/.

7 Center for the Study of Global Christianity, Frequently Asked Questions, "Is the United States Becoming Secularized?" https://www.gordonconwell.edu/center-for-global-christianity/research/quick-facts/.

8 David Masci and Gregory A. Smith, "5 Facts About US Evangelical Protestants," Pew Research Center, March 1, 2018, https://www.pewresearch.org/short-reads/2018/03/01/5-facts-about-u-s-evangelical-protestants/.

9 Center for the Study of Global Christianity, "Status of Global Christianity, 2023, in the Context of 1900–2050," https://www.gordonconwell.edu/center-for-global-christianity/resources/status-of-global-christianity/.

Chapter 6: The Inside-Out Strategy

1 To learn more about American Campfire Revival, click on "ACR" at kirkcameron.com. The broadcasts are available for free in audio form on major podcast networks.

2 "Where the body of the people, or any single man, is deprived of their right, or is under the exercise of a power without right, and have no appeal on earth, then they have a liberty to appeal to heaven, whenever they judge the cause of sufficient moment." John Locke, "Of Prerogative," book 2, chapter 14, *Two Treatises of Government*, 1689, https://www.johnlocke.net/2022/07/two-treatises-of-government-book-ii_28.html.

3 Philiana Ng, "GLAAD Fires Back After 'Growing Pains' Star Kirk Cameron Calls Homosexuality 'Unnatural,'" *The Hollywood Reporter*, March 3, 2012, https://www.hollywoodreporter.com/news/general-news/kirk-cameron-homosexuality-unnatural-glaad-296665/; but see Erin Carlson, "Piers Morgan Defends Kirk Cameron's Anti-Gay Comments as 'Brave,'" The Hollywood Reporter, March 5, 2012, https://www.hollywoodreporter.com/tv/tv-news/kirk-cameron-piers-morgan-gay-marriage-296789/#!.

4 Marshall Foster, *The American Covenant: The Untold Story* (Franklin, TN: American Covenant Press, 2021), 5.

ENDNOTES

Chapter 7: Army of Compassion

1 Marshall Foster, "When Freedom Was Only a Dream," *World History Institute Journal*, November 2014, 2.

2 Daniel Dreisbach, "The Bible and the American Founders," vol. 3, no. 3, *Broadcast Talks*, C. S. Lewis Institute, August 1, 2018, https://www.cslewisinstitute.org/wp-content/uploads/Broadcast-Talks_3.3-The-Bible-and-the-American-Founders-6598.pdf. The Founding Fathers had a particular interest in the book of Deuteronomy, which deals with Israel establishing the political and legal institutions necessary to govern a nation.

3 Harry S. Stout, *The New England Soul: Preaching and Religious Culture in Colonial New England*, 25th anniversary ed. (New York: Oxford University Press, 2011), 3.

4 C. H. Spurgeon, sermon 1831, "Smoking Flax," Metropolitan Tabernacle, London, June 1, 1884, https://www.spurgeongems.org/sermon/chs1831.pdf.

5 *Amazing Grace*, directed by Michael Apted (Walden Media, 2006).

6 Stephen Tomkins, *The Clapham Sect: How Wilberforce's Circle Changed Britain* (Oxford, UK: Lion Hudson, 2010), 11.

7 Tomkins, 248.

8 Kirk Cameron, *Still Growing: An Autobiography* (Ventura, CA: Regal, 2008), 140.

Chapter 8: The Comeback

1 *Harriet*, directed by Kasi Lemmons (Perfect World Pictures, 2019).

2 Sarah H. Bradford, *Scenes in the Life of Harriet Tubman* (Auburn, NY: Moses, 1869), 50–51.

3 Marshall Foster, "From Great Catastrophe to Great Awakening," *World History Institute Journal*, May–June 2020.

4 *The Epistle of Mathetes to Diognetus*, chaps. 5—6, Christian Classics Ethereal Library, https://ccel.org/ccel/mathetes/epistle_of_mathetes_to_diognetus/anf01.iii.ii.v.html.

5 Center for the Study of Global Christianity, "Christianity in Its Global Context, 1970–2020," June 2013, 78, https://www.gordonconwell.edu/wp-content/uploads/sites/13/2019/04/2ChristianityinitsGlobalContext.pdf.

6 Center for the Study of Global Christianity, Frequently Asked Questions, "Why Do You Report Such High Figures for Christian Martyrs?" https://www.gordonconwell.edu/center-for-global-christianity/research/quick-facts/.

7 See https://www.brielldecker.com/, https://www.shortcreekdreamcenter.org/, and the documentary *Prisoner of the Prophet* on Discovery+ for more on this story.

Acknowledgments

Chelsea—You are beautiful and brave. You are the light of my heart, my life, and my love. Your heart defines what motherhood is all about and our children are blessed by your heaven-sent love and commitment to them. You are my example of authenticity, love, and power under God's control. You have never stopped courageously valuing the things that matter most and have extended grace to me more than I deserve. Thank you for your love, for your commitment to God, me, and the kids, and for the ways in which you continue to encourage and inspire countless families. You are the one who has shown me what it means to be brave.

Dr. Marshall Foster—My brother in arms! Why did you leave so soon? We were just getting started. I'll forever be grateful to you for recruiting me into the Army of Compassion and telling me stories about the faith and courage of Patrick, the Pilgrims, Braveheart, and Longshanks! Ever since you joined the great cloud of witnesses in Heaven's balcony, I've sensed your impassioned voice speaking to me, reminding me through stories from history of God's tsunami wave of victory washing over the whole earth.

Rex Holt—My pastor, my mentor, my friend. You inspire me. You encourage me. You are a brave hero to many, but you are the third musketeer to me. Thank you for being a living example of the kind of husband, father, and Christian I want to be.

Wolgemuth & Associates—Thank you, Robert and Erik, for shepherding me through all the aspects of this book, from start to finish, with professionalism, skill, and grace.

Brave Books and Post Hill Press—Thank you, Trent, Justin, Zach, and the team at Brave Books and Post Hill for an incredible ride teaching kids about faith and courage and for believing in me enough to publish this book.

Eric Stanford—You, sir, are a scholar, a true gentleman, a real family man, and a wonderful wordsmith. Thank you for your endless hours of discussion, your excellent questions, your incredible listening and writing skills. Thank you for finding my voice and helping me speak through *Born to Be Brave*. I literally couldn't have done this without you. Thanks for challenging my ideas, embracing my vision of victory, and turning my scattered, impassioned ramblings into a readable, sensible manifesto of hope and bravery.

Jay Younts—Your white beard must be the source of your Gandalf-like wisdom. Everyone needs a true-blue friend, a guide. Someone trustworthy to offer a listening ear, to speak truth rather than just true facts, and above all else, to share wisdom from above. Thank you for your essential historical and theological help with this project.

About the Author

Kirk Cameron is known by millions as Mike Seaver from the 1980s sitcom *Growing Pains*. Since then, Kirk starred in *Fireproof*—the number-one inspirational movie of its year—and the movie *Left Behind*, based on the wildly popular series of novels of the same name. With the Kendrick Brothers, he produced the film *Lifemark*, about the beauty of adoption. He has also livestreamed *American Campfire Revival* and produced the documentaries *Monumental* and *The Homeschool Awakening*. Kirk hosts TBN's television series *Takeaways with Kirk Cameron*. He authored the memoir *Still Growing* and several children's books that teach biblical principles and character. Recently, Kirk has become a familiar figure on news outlets, where he comments on current events and urges people of faith to bring biblical values back to the forefront of our culture.

Kirk and his wife, Chelsea Noble, have been married for more than thirty years, have six grown children, and host an all-expenses-paid summer camp for terminally ill kids and their families called Camp Firefly. Kirk and Chelsea live in Tennessee.